COLLECTING
GEORGIAN AND VICTORIAN
CRAFTS

BOOKS BY JUNE FIELD

The Ordinary Man's Guide to Collecting Antiques
Creative Patchwork
Cottages and Conversions at Home and Abroad
Collecting Georgian and Victorian Crafts

COLLECTING GEORGIAN AND VICTORIAN CRAFTS

JUNE FIELD FRSA

CHARLES SCRIBNER'S SONS
NEW YORK

William Heinemann Ltd
15 Queen Street, Mayfair, London W1A 8BE
LONDON   MELBOURNE   TORONTO
JOHANNESBURG   AUCKLAND

First published 1973
© 1973 June Field FRSA

434 426240 4

A–3.73 (I)

Printed in Great Britain
Library of Congress Catalog Card Number 72–11320
SBN 684–13260–5

Contents

Acknowledgements

To the many experts – museum curators, antique dealers, collectors and authors – who have provided information for this book, my deepest thanks and appreciation. My particular appreciation must go to Barbara Morris of the Bethnal Green Museum, London, for her checking of the details in the needlework chapters.

My thanks also to the various photographers who supplied photographs for the book, with particular mention of Ross Wills and Michael Millar of Millar and Harris, who took the bulk of them.

Introduction

CRAFTS . . . What an unfortunate word! It so often conjures up images of folksy figures turning out homely offerings no one would really wish to own. Yet every so often the word comes back into fashion again, imbued with the magic of phrases like "home-made", "original", "exclusive", "individual", "one-of-a-kind", and once more crafts are acceptable, worthy of the painstaking effort that has gone into their production.

That time is now, when, weary of the mass-produced, machine-made, untouched-by-human-hand object, in a jet-age, no-time-for-leisure era, yet often with too much of it around, we are suddenly aware of the novel, interesting and sometimes beautiful and elegant things our Georgian and Victorian forbears made; things we can collect and still get pleasure from, or things we can learn how to make ourselves.

That is what this book is about. Crafts, and some of the people who made them.

Now, having said that hand-made things are desirable, I have to admit that not everything hand-made is good, and that some frightful horrors have been perpetrated in the name of craftwork! Obviously one has to be selective.

Would-be collectors of anything always want to know how other collectors got started. How did it all begin, my interest in collecting Georgian and Victorian crafts? Believe it or not, it was patchwork which sparked it off.

Back in the late 1960s there was a revival of interest in patchwork, period and modern. It ran along a whole wavelength in furnishings and fashion and the interest kept on growing with its peak still to be reached even now.

Further interest was stimulated in 1970 when I organized a Patchwork Competition and Exhibition in conjunction with the National Federation of Women's Institutes. It was sponsored by Sanderson, the company who produce fabrics and wallpapers under Royal Warrant, and was billed as "The Biggest Patchwork Exhibition in the World", bringing in over eight hundred entries, quilts, cushion covers, wall hangings, clothes, all in patchwork.

After I had started to collect patchwork, the road led to other ornamental work that one could only call "decorative fancies". How to find one's way along it? As it is difficult to learn a language solely from books – regular practice in conversation and meeting the people of the country is needed in order to become fluent – so I found that constant handling and looking at articles was required to decide which decorative fancies one should go in for.

You have to learn to pick and choose, following your own tastes. As all collectors have to do, you will also have to decide on whether you will accept a little damage in an item because it fills a gap in your collection, or whether you will stick out for only perfect goods. Of course it is always preferable to pay more and get better quality, but collections would never get started at all if one always insisted on this principle.

1

Persevere with reading and researching, and you can build up an interesting, worth-while collection of domestic craftwork at a moderate cost. What to pay? It is difficult to be specific about prices, particularly as they are continually on the rise. The only comfort is that inflation and spiralling costs make a collection more valuable as time goes on; which naturally to a collector with a true affection for what he or she buys, is only a small priority. It is obviously sensible to limit yourself at the start by having a budget, and expand as you can.

The best guide on what to pay is still to buy only what you like. If you like something it is surprising how soon you forget the cost. If you don't like it, the thing is dear at any price! It all adds up to the fact that if collecting is to be more than just accumulating, you must buy to please yourself, not follow the dictates of fashion.

Many articles in my collection were gathered at a modest cost; their major value is their charm and novelty. Naturally I also like to feel I can sell them well so that I can re-invest in different pieces if I want to.

I am not an expert in craftwork, but I am an enthusiast, an *aficionado*, an admirer of things which people both past and present have put a lot of love and effort into.

I have done an enormous amount of research, and there is still a great deal more to do; but the writing has to start some time. One is constantly gathering extra information, and much can be brought to light by other collectors learning and researching as they build up their collections.

For any errors and omissions I claim, as I did in my previous book *The Ordinary Man's Guide to Collecting Antiques*, that old business adage "E. & O.E." (errors and omissions excepted), and leave you, the reader, should you so wish, to tell me of *your* facts and finds.

1

Paper Patterns

"She had an enthusiast's zeal for continually making new experiments, the artistic instinct for discovery, or inventing the best, often very original, means of securing each particular effect, matching the medium to the material, working always direct from nature, building design from knowledge, giving it life."

Mrs Delany at Court and Among the Wits
R. BRIMLEY JOHNSON

Give an eighteenth-century girl a pair of scissors and a pot of gum and she was in her element. The art of cutting paper was in its heyday in the mid 1700s.

The only tools needed in addition to fine scissors were razor-sharp and pointed quill knives in various sizes, plus a hone and oil for continual sharpening.

Princess Elizabeth, George III's third daughter, was an ardent paper-cutter in pictures, shadow perforations and pin-pricking. She was probably taught by Mary Delany (1700–88), that original do-it-yourself craft worker of whom more in the shellwork chapter. Mrs Delany invented "paper mosaicks", which were really flowers, cut in paper and mounted on a thick piece of drawing paper washed over in Indian ink to make it a dull black, and a perfect foil for the colourful blooms.

Mrs Delany began this painstaking, finicky work at the age of seventy-two, going on until she was eighty-two, only giving up because of failing sight. Even at the age of eighty she was a sprightly soul, writing that "after this week I shall be monstrous busy, as I am under a necessity of whitewashing, new papering, and painting my drawing room. . . . Removing pictures, books and china will find me a good deal of busyness."

In the introduction to her copious published correspondence (1925 edition) Brimley Johnson wrote of these Flora Delanica (her own whimsical name for the flowers, obviously derived from Hudson's *Flora Anglica*), in glowing terms:

The delicacy of the craftsmanship is incredible; with its clear and unhesitating outline, bold curves, the minutest variation in tint, the exact character of the surface. . . .

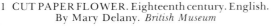

1 CUT PAPER FLOWER. Eighteenth century. English.
By Mary Delany. *British Museum*

2 CUT PAPER FLOWER. Eighteenth century. English.
By Mary Delany. *British Museum*

The design of each is a triumph of artistic convention: the composition positively startles one by its daring anticipation of the most modern examples of decorative applied art. To turn over these thousand brilliant flower-pictures is to gaze spell-bound upon bold splashes of rich colour, gossamer delicacy in vignette, strange line-harmonies we had supposed Japanese; and every subtlety of an unerring instinct for perfect grouping and composition: everywhere, life, truth and art. Since the petals, stamina, style and leaves, the lights, shades and tints were all *cut out* and laid on in place, since the veinings of leaves and the ridges of stalks are super-imposed, they have a solidity or rotund depth which gives them a radiant vitality.

Most of Mary Delany's flowers are preserved in the British Museum. They were left to the Museum in 1897 by her great-niece Lady Llanover. Go along to the Print Room and ask to see the boxes and boxes of them, all carefully labelled with the name of the plant, written in her careful, precise hand. The blush rose, China rose, magnolia, China asters, holyhock (the spelling of the time), the crimson auricula, all are there, as bright and life-like as they were over two hundred years ago.

Some twenty of the pictures were left to Queen Charlotte, which are now in the library at Windsor Castle, for they were greatly admired by King George and Queen Charlotte (in 1778 Mrs Delany observed that "the King asked me if I had added to my book of flowers, and desired he might see it").

4

3 CUT PAPER FLOWER. Eighteenth century. English. By Mary Delany. *British Museum*

4 CUT PAPER FLOWER. Eighteenth century. English. By Mary Delany. *British Museum*

Other women were also occupied in other forms of **cut paper work** (as Mrs Delany herself was at an early age), all busily snipping away at groups of figures, houses, animals, birds and the like. Lady Andover (a friend of Mrs Delany's) is said to have excelled in the cutting-out of paper figures and landscapes.

The Cecil Higgins Museum, Castle Close, in Bedford, have a charming cut-paper picture of a flowering tree in a pot with parrots on the bushes, with two winged cherubs bearing the inscription "Martha Seymour, Wantage, Berks, 1748". This could perhaps have been the Mistress Seymour who was a regular exhibitor of paper-cut pictures at the Free Society of Artists 1765–76. The catalogue shows these to have included landscapes, coats of arms and cyphers.

An enchanting paper picture which I saw for sale at a recent Grosvenor House Antiques Fair had, on the back, an elaborate history of the picture being passed from one relation to another, the original paper-cutter being Ann Cotton of Suffolk in 1770.

A fine flower picture in cut paper which was made, not by a lady of leisure, but a French prisoner-of-war, is in the Peterborough Museum. It would have been made any time between 1756 and 1815, when Frenchmen were behind bars, in Norman Cross, near Peterborough. The flowers were probably cut from ordinary drawing-paper, and varnished with some sort of liquid to preserve them.

American women were snipping away with their scissors, too, particularly in

5

5 CUT PAPER PICTURE. Mid-eighteenth century. English. A flowering tree in a pot, with parrots, and two winged cherubs bearing the inscription "Martha Seymour Wantage Berks 1748". *The Cecil Higgins Art Gallery, Castle Close, Bedford*

6 CUT PAPER PICTURE. Eighteenth century. English. A basket of flowers. Cut by Ann Cotton of Suffolk in 1770. *Mallett*

Pennsylvania. In the Henry Francis du Pont Winterthur Museum, Delaware, is a delightful Valentine in cut and painted paper. The square picture has delicate rosettes in red, blue, yellow and brown, interspersed with hearts containing messages in German, all on a black ground. In the centre a little rosette contains the name Adam Dambach Lancaster 1779. Two little love birds perch on the two hearts at the top.

Another Valentine, possibly from the same town, and the same period, includes clever superimposed cut-paper work. The main motif is a central "saw-tooth wheel" surrounded by hearts and flowers, all hand-coloured in polychrome hues. The flower-strewn name is Dinah McFadgen.

There is obviously a spot of patriotism about a cut-paper picture with a half sewn and half cut foliate border encircling a spread eagle with the American flag bearing eleven stars behind its head. "Liberty" is the slogan at the top.

Possibly the prettiest paper-work picture in the Winterthur Museum is one with a pencilled inscription on the back reading "Mary Godchalk 1840". It is in a deep rectangular box frame with a glass front, the interior lined with white paper. The wide border of vivid green paper surrounds brightly coloured flowers of fluted, circular paper. In the middle is a tree with a fabric bird sitting on it.

Back in Britain, in the 1830s, there was the work of a talented invalid, Amelia Blackburn. Her efforts, appropriately called Amelias, were a complicated form of

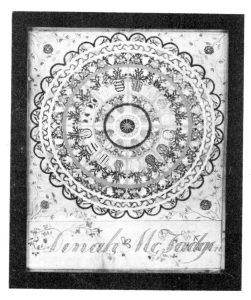

7 CUT PAPER VALENTINE. Eighteenth century. American. In cut and painted paper, with the centre rosette containing the inscription "Adam Dambach Lancaster 1779". *The Henry Francis du Pont Winterthur Museum*

8 CUT PAPER VALENTINE. 1790–1840. American. The central motif is a "saw-tooth" wheel, bordered with hearts and flowers, and the name Dinah McFadgen. *The Henry Francis du Pont Winterthur Museum*

10 CUT PAPER PICTURE. Nineteenth century. American. A wide border of vivid green paper surrounds brightly coloured flowers of fluted paper. In the centre a fabric bird. Pencilled inscription on the back reads "Mary Godchalk 1840". *The Henry Francis du Pont Winterthur Museum*

9 CUT PAPER PICTURE. 1780–1800. American. This patriotic offering has a half sewn and half cut border encircling an eagle with the American flag, topped with the "Liberty" slogan. *The Henry Francis du Pont Winterthur Museum*

11 PIN-PRICK PICTURE. Mid-nineteenth century. English. Cut paper bird, snake and tree, with raised effects obtained from pin-pricks at the back of the paper. The work of Amelia Blackburn. *British Museum*

paper mosaics, with raised effects obtained from **pin-pricking** from the back of white, hand-made paper.

First the basis of the design was cut out and mounted. This was a comparatively simple outline such as a branching tree or the leafy stems of a garland. Then the really clever work followed, when the main features of the design were added – exotic birds, animals and foliage, fish among water weeds, and so on. All these were constructed feather by feather, petal by petal; each tiny detail, whether it was a leaf or blade of grass, sometimes so minute as to be almost invisible, was cut out separately and gummed into position, often each line no thicker than a hair.

Every cutting was vividly coloured and shaded. Pin-pricking from the back was carried out when knives and scissors could not produce the desired effect. Only by closely looking at the completed picture can one see the tiny spaces dividing one line from another; the whole effect is of delicate brushwork.

8

Hibiscus Rosa Sinensis
China Rose

12 CUT PAPER FLOWER. Eighteenth century. English. By Mary Delany. *British Museum*

13 PIN-PRICK PICTURE. Nineteenth century. English. Called "The Mother's Hope", the fabric of the dresses is cleverly suggested by closely grouped minute piercing from the back. Probably copied from an engraving by T. Palser 1815. *Radio Times Hulton Picture Library*

14 PIN-PRICK PICTURE. Nineteenth century. English. The same subject as a mezzotint printed for Carrington Bowles "Ha! Ha! Ha! I've Got The Chink", which is printed in the reverse direction. *British Museum*

15 PIN-PRICK PICTURE. Nineteenth century. English. Birds on a tree.
Radio Times Hulton Picture Library

16 FILIGREE AND ROLLED PAPER WORK. *c.* 1710. English. A wax model of Queen Anne. The Queen's robe is entirely composed of minute rolls of stiffened paper, and she stands against a background of pillars and draperies all made in the same way. *The Lady Lever Art Gallery, Port Sunlight*

17 CABINET COVERED IN ROLLED PAPER FILIGREE. 1780. English. The cabinet and stand are completely covered with a mosaic of the filigree work. *The Lady Lever Art Gallery, Port Sunlight*

One of these beautiful cut-paper pictures by Amelia Blackburn can be seen in the British Museum.

The type of pins used for pin-pricking were steel needles fixed immovably in short handles, coming in sizes from fine to coarse. With these one could work intricate compositions requiring holes of several sizes.

Costumes could be made quite elaborate by a pin-pricker with a good eye for design and three needles. Folds and creases were reproduced by wide bands pierced with a large pin from the front at regular intervals. The fabric of the dress was cleverly suggested by closely grouped minute piercing from the back done in such a way as to cause a slightly embossed effect accentuated by unpierced portions.

An attractive example is shown by what is probably an early nineteenth-century pin-pricked picture called "The Mother's Hope", with a mother and child (probably a boy!) garbed in the high-waisted dresses of the Regency days. Some of this pin-prick work was of the same subject as current engravings and mezzotints, and this was probably derived from *Mother's Pride* published in 1815 by T. Palser. In the British Museum is a pin-prick picture from a mezzotint printed for Carrington Bowles, "Ha! Ha! Ha! I've got the Chink", which is printed in the reverse direction.

The most detailed method of "Piercing Costumes on Paper" is fully described in *The Young Ladies' Book by A. Lady* (1829):

11

18 WORK BOX DECORATED ROLLED PAPER. Seventeenth century. English. The centre panel is filled with shells and a paper bird, and the initials MW (for Mary Wright), and the date 1687 form part of the over-all design. *Victoria and Albert Museum*

19 TEA CADDY DECORATED ROLLED PAPER. Eighteenth century. English. The initials WER and the date 1797 are all worked in rolled paper. *H. C. Baxter*

Turkish and other figures in Oriental costume were produced by a combination of water colour painting for the features, with a series of small punctures made with needles of various sizes for the dresses. . . . The face, hands and feet being first drawn and coloured, the outlines and folds of drapery are marked with a tracing needle; the paper is then laid upon a piece of smooth cloth or a few sheets of blotting paper and the punctures inserted in the folds of the dress from the front to the back of the paper; the drawing is then laid with its surface downwards and the interior of the various outlines filled up with punctures made with a very fine needle from the back to the front of the paper.

Pin-prick pictures of various subjects can still be found by the collector, even if they are only simple ones of birds on a tree; they still reveal the intricate technique.

Another fascinating form of paper creativeness is the work done in parchment or stiff paper known to every eighteenth-century woman from Mary Delany to Jane Austen as *filigree* and *rolled paper work*. In Miss Austen's *Sense and Sensibility* (published 1811) Elinor Dashwood offered to roll the papers for Lucy Steel when she was making a filigree basket.

Even much earlier, in 1663, Samuel Pepys speaks of a basket made of paper fili-gree, and across the Atlantic in 1710 filigree work was being taught in Boston private schools.

Women could receive instruction in how to roll narrow strips of paper into shapes to suggest fine wood chip carving, which would then have one edge glued to a back-ground of paper or silk-covered wood. When the papers were coloured and gilded and cut very fine to form lacework spirals they resembled delicate gold and silver wire filigree.

A fine example of filigree work is the wax model of Queen Anne, *c.* 1710, in the Lady Lever Art Gallery in Port Sunlight, Cheshire. The Queen's robe is entirely com-posed of minute rolls of stiffened paper set horizontally, and she stands against a background of pillars and draperies all made in the same way. The "filigree" is

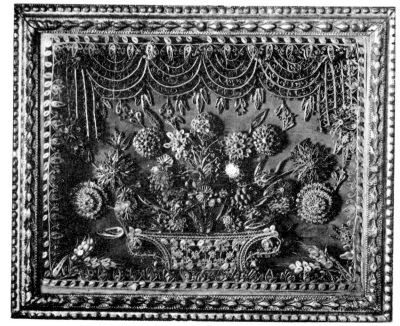

20 ROLLED AND CUT PAPER FLOWER PICTURE. *c.* 1700. English. Bowl of flowers in cut and rolled paper. *H. C. Baxter*

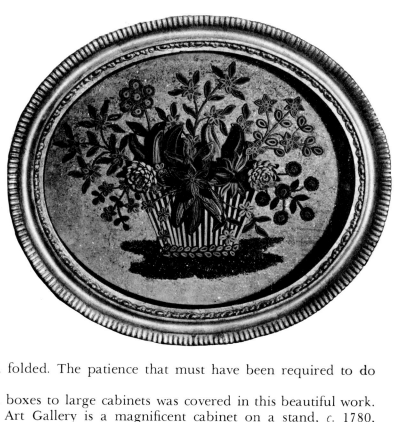

21 ROLLED AND CUT PAPER FLOWER PICTURE. Early eighteenth century. Basket of flowers in cut and rolled paper. *Glaisher & Nash*

exquisitely coloured and folded. The patience that must have been required to do all this!

Everything from small boxes to large cabinets was covered in this beautiful work. Also in the Lady Lever Art Gallery is a magnificent cabinet on a stand, *c.* 1780,

22 QUILL WORK CANDLE SCONCE. 1730–1750. American. On the back of the box an aged label reads Abby L. Osgood. The glass candle arm does not appear to be original to the quill work box. The candle arm bracket was replaced in September 1958 and electrified. *Henry Francis du Pont Winterthur Museum*

23 CUT PAPER WORK. *c.* nineteenth century. Bruin the bear and his feather surround is cut from a tiny watch paper. The detail is incredible. This photograph is enlarged—the real size is that of the back of a watch. *British Museum*

almost completely covered with a mosaic of rolled-paper filigree work, from its long, elegant, tapering legs to the facings of the numerous little drawers and tiny "hide-away" cupboards in the interior of the cabinet. The decoration of birds, foliage, flowers and swags are all "carved" from paper, and form a frame for the hand-painted panels set in the doors.

There is a fascinating work-box in the Victoria and Albert Museum showing how rolled-paper-work could embellish quite an ordinary-looking wooden box. The top and sides of yellow silk are decorated with hearts and flowers in cut paper painted and gilded. A centre panel is filled with shells and a paper bird, and worked in the overall design are the initials MW (for Mary Wright) and the date 1687.

The date and the owner's initials were often worked into a box, which can be a guide-line to a collector. A fine tea-caddy I saw in a private collection has the initials WER and the date 1797.

An enormous number of boxes was being decorated in the eighteenth century, the box being supplied "in the rough" by cabinet-makers, with shallow depressions in each panel to take the paper-work. In 1791 Princess Elizabeth was supplied with one by Charles Elliott, royal furniture-maker to George III. It was a box made for filigree work with ebony moulding, lock and key, lined inside and out. With the box came fifteen ounces of different filigree papers and an ounce of gold paper, to carry out the decoration.

If you should be lucky enough to come across a decorated box that, while still beautifully and skilfully decorated, has rather crude hinges, poor quality paper lining, and no lavish gilt handles or moulding, then it would also have been made by one of those afore mentioned French prisoners-of-war who ended up in the gaols of Britain while fighting in the Napoleonic wars. (Read more about their craftsmanship in the next chapter, in the straw-work section.)

Intricate flower pictures were also made in rolled paper, and these can still be found by a persevering collector. I have seen a very ornate one dated around 1700, and a later Regency one, much simpler, but equally effective, in an oval frame.

Another variation of paper-work was rolled-paper **quill work**, in which various other interesting materials were interspersed – beads, feathers and pine for instance.

Quill-work candle sconces can be seen at the Henry Francis du Pont Winterthur Museum; one comes from Massachusetts (1730–50) and the design forms a vase of flowers and leaves with two seated lambs; the other, of the same vintage, perhaps a little earlier, is believed to be European in origin, and the aged label on the back reads "Abby L. Osgood".

Coats-of-arms in **cut vellum** were also a craze of the mid eighteenth century. One of its leading professional exponents was Nathaniel Bermingham, described in *Mortimer's Director* in 1763 as

> Herald Painter and improver of the curious art of cutting out Portraits and Coats of Arms in Vellum, with the points of a pen-knife . . . Specimens of his peculiar talent may be seen at his house, the corner of Great Queen Street, opposite Long Acre.

In 1774 Bermingham exhibited his "peculiar talent" at the Society of Artists, a portrait of the Duke of Gloucester, "cut in paper in an entirely new manner". One of his cut-paper pictures of Frederick, Prince of Wales (father of George III), is in the Victoria and Albert Museum. Specimens of his work emerge for sale from time to time, as well as those from the do-it-yourself brigade at home who, naturally, were also having a go at the curious art.

The *New Lady's Magazine* for 1786 issued a series of twelve sheets of patterns showing them how to do it.

A Mrs Seymour, whom I referred to earlier in the cut-paper section, cut "a frame of various devices in vellum with scissors, containing the Lord's Prayer, with her name, date of the month and year, in the compass of a silver three-pence – a most extraordinary feat".

Landscapes cut in paper were at the 1851 Great Exhibition at Crystal Palace, that brainchild of Queen Victoria's husband, Prince Albert, which produced so much that was good and bad in the arts of the times.

An article in the *Expositer* for 1851 refers to "some beautiful specimens of cutting in paper, in imitation of nature". These were by F. Windsor, the profile artist at the Royal Polytechnic Institute.

24 CUT PAPER FLOWERS. A bunch of flowers cut so naturally in paper, they look like real pressed flowers. *British Museum*

"*Respectfully dedicated to Miss Becker & the strong minded sisterhood as a prophetic illustration of the relative position of the sexes, in the coming*

"*I had a little Husband no bigger than my Thumb, I put him on a quart pot, & there I bid him drum.*"

25 CUT SILHOUETTE WORK. *c.* 1870. English. Figures cut by Jane E. Cook from white paper given extra interest by pin-pricking and embossing. *British Museum*

In the album of cut-paper work in the British Museum there are tiny watch papers cut into exquisite, lace-like shapes, all in the minute space of the back of a watch – a small one at that.

Also in the book is a delightful bunch of paper flowers, so delicately cut and coloured they look the real thing.

One cannot leave the craft of paper-cutting without referring to the studies in **silhouette**, now more commonly called profiles. I am not going to go into long details of this fascinating subject – there is an impressive list of books by expert collectors of long standing on professional profilists. But from the mid eighteenth century the art of silhouette-cut pictures was also a hobby for amateurs, lasting well into mid-Victorian times.

Once again, George III's daughter Elizabeth was well to the fore, snipping away at portraits of her parents and allegorical subjects. In 1802 Henry Edridge painted the Princess seated in a window, scissors in hand, engaged in her favourite hobby of cutting silhouettes from paper.

A delightful collection of figure paper-work came from Jane E. Cook (*née* Robins), wife of Henry Cook the headmaster of King Alfred's Grammar School, Wantage, fortunately preserved for posterity in a little green bound album in the Print Room of the British Museum. It contains a number of original cuttings in white paper on black, with amusing little rhymes written underneath them.

Obviously a forerunner of Women's Lib (even in the 1870s), she wrote of one enchanting vignette as "respectfully dedicated to Miss Becker and the strong minded sisterhood as a prophetic illustration of the relative position of the sexes in the coming time".

Underneath the figures, not only cut from white paper, but given extra interest by pin-pricking and embossing, goes the refrain:

16

26 SILHOUETTE
CUTTING.
Contemporary.
American. *Joseph Mendez
at the New York Flea
Market*

"I had a little Husband no bigger than my Thumb,
I put him on a quart pot, and there I bid him drum."

For more details of the numerous amateur, yet no-less-skilled profilists, I recommend the reading of F. Gordon Roe's admirable *Women in Profile* – it reveals a wealth of research into the lives of these talented women.

The art is still very much alive today, as you can see if you visit the New York Flea Market – "Silhouettes done here by Joseph Mendez" goes a sign.

17

2

Texture Is All

FEATHERED FRIENDS – BIRD PICTURES,
FEATHER FLOWERS, AND JUST BIRDS
WAX FLOWERS AND FRUIT
STRAW AND CORK WORK

"Fine feathers make fine birds"

English Proverb
J. RAY

My first bird buys were two fine **bird feather pictures**, a pair of handsome pheasants in maple frames, flamboyant and arrogant as they perch on the painted boughs, their long, protruding tail feathers sweeping the ground.

Their speckled brown feathers, with a pinky or bluish tinge according to the light, are in remarkably good condition, their texture clean and colours bright. Whether they have been touched up or added to I don't know, but they are a spectacular pair.

How were the bird pictures made? Mainly, the birds were drawn on a plain green- or cream-washed paper and filled in with the appropriate coloured feathers, which were gummed on, starting from the tail and building towards the neck. They were either small birds, blue tits, yellow-hammers, canaries, thrushes and so on, or the larger pheasants and partridges. A glass bead was often used for the eye that showed, as the birds were usually made up sideways on.

Feathers form part of the decoration of à la Ronde, Exmouth, the remarkable round house built by the Misses Parminter in the Italian style in the 1790s after they returned from a holiday in Italy; you can read more about it in chapter three, in the section on shellwork. It is sufficient to say here that richly feathered birds alternate with shell panels in the gallery that runs round the inner wall at the top of the house.

At Arlington Court, Barnstaple, Devon, also mentioned in the shellwork chapter, the lobby leading off the gallery in the house has textured panels too, each with six exotic birds made up in feathers mounted on paper. These are the work of Lady Rosamond Christie, of Tapely Park, Instow, a cousin of the last owner Miss Rosalie Chichester, and the mother of John Christie, the founder of Glyndebourne Opera House.

Contemporary bird feather pictures are around for the collector, too. In the Grosvenor Gallery in London you can see the work of Arturo Cavalli, an Italian artist. His

27 FEATHER PICTURES; Nineteenth century. A brace of pheasants complete with long, sweeping feathers; in maple frames on painted boughs and foliage. *E. Tudor-Hart. Author's collection*

"L'Uovo", done in 1967, is great fun, an oil on canvas with a "body" of ostrich feathers.

But back to our decorative feather workers of Georgian days; the craft was being taught in the needlework schools of Britain and Boston as early as 1716, and needless to say Mary Delany was involved in working with feathers. In 1727 she sent her sister Anne "a tippet of her own making and invention", Brimley Johnson, in a footnote to her writing, refers to it as having feathers in it – "those of the macaw, dark blue gentianello colour, relieved with scarlet, and interspersed with small feathers of the canary birds".

In the nineteenth century feathers were collected and made into **flowers** by bending or curling them with a penknife and wiring them. Some flowers were made into wreaths and put under the ubiquitous glass case, others were used as bouquets in vases.

Books of the period gave precise instructions on how to clean feathers of their animal oil; quicklime mixed with water to make limewater, was the main ingredient;

28 FEATHER PICTURE. Early nineteenth century. A bird complete with feathers perched on a painted bough. *Mallett*

29 FEATHER PICTURE; Nineteenth century. A bird, complete with feathers, on a painted bough. Framed in maple. *Ingram Warwick Antique Lovers' Coterie*

20

30 FEATHER PICTURE. Nineteenth century. A bird, complete with feathers, on a painted bough. *Mallett*

31 BIRD PICTURE. Twentieth century. Italian. "L'Uovo" by Arturo Cavalli. Oil and ostrich feathers on canvas *Grosvenor Gallery*

32 WAX FRUIT. Victorian. English. A basket of wax fruit: on the ground a basket of Berlin wool work flowers (see Chapter 9). *Harris Museum and Art Gallery, Preston*

to clean white ostrich feathers, four ounces of white soap, cut small, was dissolved in four pints of hot water, and beaten up into a lather. The feathers were dunked in and out of the mixture for about five minutes, and then washed in very hot clean water. A final cold rinse and a shake near the fire until dry completed the process.

The dry feathers would be recurled by using a narrow paper-knife, drawing each fibre of the feather over the edge of the knife while holding it by finger and thumb.

Victorian fancy workers also cut ordinary goose feathers in the shape of petals and leaves. The Chester Historical Society, West Chester, in the USA has a framed confection of them, dyed, painted, and curled, forming a pretty floral arrangement.

Feathers for making feather flowers and rosettes were often dyed different colours. Beeton's *All About Everything* of the 1890s commented:

Those which have naturally no decided tint may be improved in colour taking care to use the dye which comes nearest to their natural tints. . . . The first thing necessary is to put the feathers into hot water for a few seconds, and to let them drain before they are put into the dyes.

Among the popular colours used were:

Green – indigo liquid was mixed with turmeric with boiling water poured over the lot and the feathers put into simmer until they acquired the depth of colour needed.

22

WAX FLOWER MODELLING.—THE WHITE CLEMATIS.

THERE is hardly a prettier
the clematis, with its snow-
centre; its perfume, too, is
be conceived. It forms taste-
summer-houses, making them
wax the clematis looks very
and if mingled with a few
gether with a yellow hearts-
a few rosebuds with their
in a thin-stemmed glass vase,
the boudoir. The materials
about 3 sheets of double white
of light yellow green wax for
the leaves, and 2 sheets of a
green for the leaves. A small
powder, and the same of white

climber to be met with than
white petals and green-tinted
one of the sweetest that can
ful arches, and covers our
look like fairy bowers. In
pretty. It is easy to model;
sprigs of forget-me-nots, to-
ease, a pink carnation, and
green leaves, placed tastefully
would form a sweet group for
for a nice-sized sprig would be
wax for the blossoms, 2 sheets
the stems, buds, and backs of
bright but rather dark yellow
quantity of Chinese white in
bloom, a small quantity of

very light green powder, a cake of purple lake, and about 2 yards of very fine silk-covered
wire; great care should be taken in choosing the wire fine enough, for the whole grace of the
sprig depends upon the neatness of the stems. A fine sable and a medium-sized camel's hair
brush, together with a very small moulding pin, finishes the list. Commence by taking the
natural flower very carefully to pieces, then take one of the 4 petals which form the outer
part of the flower, and placing it upon thick white paper, cut it out very carefully; then place
the paper pattern, which we will call No. 3, upon the double white wax, and cut out clearly for
each blossom 4 petals, making some of them smaller than others to vary the flowers. When
done, bloom the petals on both sides with a mixture of the Chinese white and bloom, taking
care not to paint quite to the base, or they will not adhere in making up. After they are all
bloomed, mould each by pressing the pin down the centre and on either side of it, so as to
form three lines; this must be done very carefully, or the petals will break; when done, give
to each one bloom more, and place them on one side in their separate lots, so that the different
sized petals for the large and small flowers may be easily got at. To make up the flower, take
a strip of the wire and mould round it a very narrow strip of green wax to just cover the wire
for the stem; when done, turn one end a little way down, and press on at its point 6 very
narrow strips of white wax of about a quarter of an inch in length; and after painting each
carefully with the green powder mixed in weak gum-water, slightly turn each point back at the
top to form the pistil. The stamens are of two sizes—the small, which we will call No. 1, and
which measures about a quarter of an inch, and the next size, which measures about half the
length again, we will call No. 2; they can be either formed from two narrow slips of wax, or
they can be made of fine white cotton, covering it with wax; the latter way is the stronger,
and although a little more trouble, it will well repay it in the end; but one thing must be borne
in mind, and that is that they must be as fine as possible. Of No. 1, which is the small size,
there should be 16, and of No. 2 there should be the same number; and whichever way they are
formed 4 of each size will have to be painted carefully with the sable brush and green mixture
as before, leaving the remainder white, and only tinting the points of each with straw colour,
which can be produced by mixing a very small portion of yellow powder with some Chinese
white. When all the stamens are cut out and arranged, press them on in rows of 8 round the
base of the pistil, first the small size, and then the large; then, with the point of the pin,
regulate them according to nature, and at their base press on at stated distances the four
petals cut from No. 1, and slightly turn them back towards the stem. The buds should be
formed of a solid piece of white wax after the shape of a grain of rice, but not quite so pointed
at the ends; the stem should be formed the same as for the flower, and the bud should be
tinted in shade according to the size of it; the very small ones should be painted all green,
and just tinted at the points with the lake mixed with the green; the larger buds should be
almost white, and the centre of the small and opening blossoms should bear more of the green
tint than the larger ones. The leaves should be formed from the real ones out of three thicknesses of green wax, and their edges should be cut out sharp and clear. The sprig should be
made up from nature if possible.

33 WAX FLOWER MODELLING. Mid-nineteenth century. English. *The Ladies' Book of the
Month*, 1867 gave full details on how to model the white clematis.

Red – a tablespoon of prepared cochineal was mixed with a teaspoonful of cream of tartar and dissolved in a quart of boiling water to which a few drops of muriate of tin were added.

Yellow – turmeric was mixed with boiling water; the addition of soda would turn the mixture orange.

About 1850, fans of coloured feathers became fashionable, and were known as "Cora" fans. Late in the century large ostrich fans came on the scene, and also exotic fans made of peacock feathers. The sticks were made from ivory, and the feathers arranged so that the "eyes" of the tail feathers formed the stick terminals. The feathered leaf was finished with a hand-painted scene.

Stuffed birds had their place in Georgian and Victorian décor too. In the eighteenth century rare birds and fauna were brought back by sailors and troops serving overseas. They were greatly in demand from those with an interest in natural history, and in 1851 the display of stuffed barn owls made the rather macabre science of taxidermy respectable.

Birds were mounted on plinths to give as natural an appearance as possible, and over the top went a domed glass case. Handsome snowy owls and rare golden eagles are extremely collectable. Sometimes a duck would be mounted in its "natural" surroundings, on a weedy sand dune, and encased in a square glass box.

Really quite attractive were groupings of brilliantly plumed birds surrounded by coloured ferns and foliage.

Collecting stuffed birds is only just coming back into fashion, and if they appeal to you, then get started now, while single unmounted birds can be bought for quite a modest sum.

It is difficult to date examples, unless a date is given on the mount. In general the more naturalistic creations are of a later date, as the technique of preserving the colour in the plumage was not used until about the 1880s. Dull feathers could be evidence of an early age.

As Beeton's dictionary of useful information and everyday information reminds us: "The beauty of stuffed birds depends much on their being well shot." It then goes on to describe in detail how the bird should be stuffed. I think the description of what happens to the "bleeding orifice" is all a little much for me to linger on!

Wax flowers and **fruit** can be things of beauty because of their realistic texture. or rather a horror. I saw some at a Christie's auction sale recently, and three groups in glass cases went for £16 or so (less than 50 dollars), and quite frankly they were in the horror class. Perhaps the fact that they had been in store in a museum contributed to their general rather unattractive and musty air. Yet wax-flower modelling was a most accomplished art in the 1800s, and after the public saw a whole section devoted to wax modelling at the Great Exhibition in 1851, great was the demand to learn how to do it.

To be credible, wax flowers had to be as lifelike as possible, and flowers of good size were pulled apart and used as patterns.

Frances Lichten in her *Decorative Art of Victoria's Era* sums up their workmanship in very appropriate style:

34 MATERIALS FOR WAX, FRUIT AND FLOWER MODELLING. As advertised by J. Barnard & Son, 339 Oxford Street, W.1. *The Ladies' Book of the Month 1867*

Those who devoted long hours to the fabrication of the waxen blossoms regarded their work not merely as a craft but as an important art form, one that partook not only of the qualities of sculpture and modelling, but of painting as well. The art required deftness, patience, observation, and artistic ability, for only those wax flowers were considered successful which imitated nature so closely that the beholder was actually deceived into thinking them real.

She who could also reproduce nature's accidentals — the bruise on a pear, the bee in the throat of a blossom, the browning edge of a leaf — was credited with displaying not only playful caprice but a high degree of artistry as well.

Big names in the wax world were Mrs Strickland, who produced a marvellous model of the *Victoria Regia* water lily in every stage of its development for displaying at the Great Exhibition; Mrs Emma Peachey, described as "artiste to Her Majesty", who wrote *The Royal Guide to Wax Flower Modelling* and who gave a private exhibition of wax flowers and fruit at her home at the same time as the Crystal Palace venture; and the Mintorns, John and Horatio, who specialized in waxwork mourning wreaths, and also provided patterns and moulds for fruit and flowers, as well as a handbook for modelling wax flowers.

The Ladies' Book of the Month (1867) gave instructions on how to make a white clematis, that "pretty climber with its snow-white petals and green-tinted centre . . . that forms tasteful arches and covers our summer houses, making them look like fairy bowers".

The materials needed to model this glamorous flower were given as three sheets of double white wax for the blossoms, two sheets of light yellow green wax for the stems, buds and backs of the leaves, and two sheets of bright but rather dark yellow green for the leaves. In addition one needed various powdered colours, two yards of very fine silk-covered wire, camel's hair brushes, and moulding pins, sticks which gave support to the flowers and made a centre for the stamens.

All these items could be purchased through J. Barnard & Son, 339 Oxford Street, W. The wax cost six shillings a gross of sheets, assorted colours, or in a block three shillings a pound; curling pins were two shillings a dozen, and moulding tools four shillings to nine shillings, according to whether they were made in boxwood or ivory. "Frost, Bloom, Down and Every Other Requisite" were available for making waxen

35 STRAW WORK. Mid-eighteenth century. English. Flower picture made from straw mounted on wire, in a contemporary lacquer frame. *Mallett*

fruit and flowers, and you could send for *The Art of Modelling and Making Wax Flowers,* by Charles Peppers, for one shilling and sixpence.

There is still a certain amount of wax modelling around for the collector, but quality is everything. Some of the fruit compositions are finely done and worth collecting as specimens of Victorian workmanship; and if you can pick up odd items of wax food (before the art died out in the 1880s, wax modelling took on a new look, that of provoking appetite), then you can make up your own groupings. After all, realistic displays of edibles in wax on the dining-table must be one-upmanship on our current offerings in plastics.

In 1703 a woman from London advertised in the *Edinburgh Gazette* that she taught pictorial **straw work**, and I have seen a beautiful English flower picture made from straw mounted on wire, probably mid eighteenth century. The flowers are exquisite in detail, with each petal separately cut. Some have a "feather-cut" edge, others are furled and folded like ribbon. I should think this is an extremely rare picture.

Another version of **straw work** is the craft brought to England from the Continent

26

36 CORK WORK. Picture in cork with buildings, trees and foliage all cut from cork. *Ingram*
Warwick Antique Lovers' Coterie

37 STRAW WORK. Late eighteenth century. A work box made by a French prisoner-of-war. Even the tiny lids to the compartments of the box frame have pictures worked in strips of straw on them. The colouring is pink and green. There is a crude mirror in the lid of the box. *Antique Supermarket. Author's collection*

late in the seventeenth century, when wood marquetry on furniture was popular. Flattened filaments of oaten or wheaten straw was split and glued on to a wooden object to be decorated, as in marquetry. This straw inlay with its arrangement of radiating lines and feather banding is particularly attractive, with the pinks and greens of the dyed straw shimmering and glinting in the light, not unlike the mosaic effects of Tunbridge Ware, which is made up of different coloured woods.

The majority of finely decorated small work available to collectors today, such as tea caddies, trinket boxes, silk holders and so on, was made by the French prisoners-of-war in Britain between 1765 and 1815. They obtained striking effects on the objects they made, often without adding any colours, merely by changing the direction of the straw and getting a difference of light and shade.

In the Peterborough Museum a whole gallery is devoted to a marvellous exhibition of a great variety of the work of these men, who were not professional soldiers, but mainly craftsmen conscripted into Napoleon's wars. They were allowed to barter or sell their handicrafts in order to supplement the meagre rations allowed them.

Jane Toller, who has made a special study of French prisoner-of-war work, des-

38 STRAW WORK. Eighteenth century. Boxes decorated with straw by French prisoners-of-war. The effect is of marquetry work in furniture. *Harrods Collectors Room*

cribes the various ways of inlaying with straw in her book *Prisoners-Of-War Work 1756–1815*.

They are:

Marquetry, pure and simple, in which wooden veneers are replaced by straw.

Mosaic, composed of tiny pieces of differently coloured straw, each piece being cut and fitted to its neighbour.

Embossing, achieved by building up the design with strips of superimposed straw.

Cementing, delicately perforated traceries of straw stuck to the article.

Cloisonné, made by gluing enormous numbers of tiny, short straws of different colours to the ground work.

Pictures were made up in straw, copied from contemporary prints, tiny fragments of split straw being glued into figure groups and landscapes; a straw marquetry view of Forde Abbey, Dorset, from a drawing by Prideaux, was used as a panel inside a lid of a superb casket made by one of the prisoners. This work is unsigned, but in the Victoria and Albert Museum and the Peterborough Museum there is some signed work by a Corporal Jean de la Porte.

Straw work boxes and caskets can still be found by enterprising collectors, although you have to be prepared to accept a little damage, as some of the straw may have shrunk away from the edges through being chipped or knocked in the course of general wear and tear. To prevent further disintegration a coat of copal varnish is recommended.

Implements for straw work must be around for collectors too. For instance there were straw-splitters, for splitting the straw into several pieces, and straw crushers.

A straw-splitter is a pear-shaped wooden instrument about four inches high, containing four or five round holes. Into these holes were fitted wheels with a varying number of sharp, radiating spokes. Each whole straw was then pulled through these wheels, and so one piece of straw could be cut into several pieces at once.

29

Straw-plaiting was done in the cottages in the early nineteenth century, and to prepare the straw for the work is had to be flattened by being crushed through a hand-roller. The roller, which has a beechwood frame and a pair of hardwood rollers, was fixed upright to the edge of a table by means of a wooden screw that passed through the table from below. It looked rather like a baby mangle from the illustration of a straw crusher in Gertrude Jekyll's *Old West Surrey, Some Notes and Memories of British Cottage Life*, published in 1904, a delightful book which includes a chapter on home industries.

Straw-plaiting, incidentally (used as braids for bonnets), was also done by the prisoners, competing so successfully with the local workers that the authorities soon put a stop to it. Raids on the prison barracks to seize hat braids for burning were frequent; but under-the-counter plaiting still went on, and even the hats and bonnets themselves were made in prison.

The British straw-plaiters, spread over Bedfordshire, Buckinghamshire and Hertfordshire, also made charming wax figures, dressed entirely in clothes made from braids of various kinds. These were grouped together and placed under a glass dome, and some can be seen at the Wardown Museum in Luton.

Also for collectors to look out for are the decorative Victorian sun shades and parasols, ornamented with split rye straw, which were often made in Italy.

Straw hassocks, laced with leather, split cane or bramble, can still be found in remote churches in Britain, and straw even found its way into lace-making. A piece of horse-hair lace with straw leaves and straw plait sewn into the design was on show at the 1851 Exhibition.

The corn dolly, that straw ornament which dates back from pagan times, made from the corn of the last sheaf, and meant to preserve the spirit of the corn mother when the corn was cut, is a fine example of decorative straw work; it still survives throughout many countries.

Modern straw work still goes on. To find out more about it, refer to *Decorative Straw Work and Corn Dollies* by Lettice Sandford and Philla Davis.

Modelling in *cork* was another favourite Victorian pastime. Cathedrals and castles were a popular subject. A. Ingram (1855–1935), a sailor who was also a craftsman and artist, and came from South Shields, produced cork pictures of Durham Cathedral and St George's Chapel at Windsor Castle.

As far as I can tell, cork sheets, cork raspings and old bottle corks were used to form buildings, trees and foliage. A turn-of-the-century edition of the invaluable *Enquire Within Upon Everything* tells you how to model caves in cork:

Construct the framework of wood, and fill up the outline with old bottle corks. The various projections, recesses and other minutiae, must be affixed afterwards with glue, after being formed of cork, or hollowed out in the necessary parts, either by burning with a hot wire and scraping it afterwards, or by means of a sharp pointed bradawl. Various parts of the model must be touched up with oil, water, or varnish colours; and powdered brick, slate and chopped lichen, or moss, dusted on.

30

3

Call of the Sea

MRS DELANY CONTINUED
SHELLS IN PICTURES, HEARTS AND FLOWERS
SHELLS IN FIGURES, FURNISHINGS AND GROTTOES

". . . running wild after shells"

Mrs Delany at Court and Among the Wits
R. BRIMLEY JOHNSON

You do not have to be a conchologist, someone who studies the nature of shells and their inhabitants, to be interested in them. Just to hear the sound of the beautiful names – angel's wing, Florida cone, long-spined star – conjures up the magic of the sea and faraway places. All these are rare shells, sometimes used in **shellwork**, that attractive craft high on the list of pastimes practised by Georgian and Victorian womenfolk.

Some shells were collected on the English sea shore, but as *The Girl's Home Companion* (a book of pastimes in work and play edited by a Mrs Valentine probably at the turn of the present century) admitted, it really needed "a naval relation to bring home a precious basket of beautiful shells".

One of the most noted shell-workers of Georgian times was of course that do-it-yourself enthusiast, Mary Delany.

This is not a book about this gossipy, but kind-hearted and industrious talented personality of the eighteenth century, but inevitably you will be reading quite a bit about her because of her remarkable skills in making so many of the things I am writing about.

In her long and detailed memoirs, Mary Delany wrote in 1734:

I have got a new madness, I am running wild after shells. This morning I have set my little collection of shells in nice order in my cabinet, and they look so beautiful, that I must by some means enlarge my stock; the beauties of shells are as infinite as of flowers. . . .

Collecting shells inevitably led to her making things with them. In 1745 she wrote:

I have been sorting my mosses and ores, and am going to arrange my shells, and to cover two large vases for my garden.

31

BLUNT GAPER (*Mya truncata*).

pretty freely, and generally live in the sand. To them belong the delicate *Tellina*—little pink shells, like scattered petals of fairy roses, to be found

BLUNT TELLEN (*Tellina crassa*).   PORCELAIN TELLEN (*Tellina tenuis*).

on our shores, and the beautiful Sunset Tellen, with alternate rays of soft sulphur and red, just like an evening sky. And above all, here is the great family of *Venus*—beautiful rounded smooth shells, closing resolutely, some

BANDED VENUS SHELL.   WART VENUS SHELL.

of brilliantly tinted enamel, some beautifully chiselled and frilled, their sculpture always following the line of the shell.

39 SHELLS. From *The Girl's Home Companion* edited by Mrs Valentine at the turn of the century.

40 MARY DELANY 1700–88. A portrait painted by J. Opie when she was in her seventies and still active in her craft work. *National Portrait Galley*

This was after her second marriage in 1743 to a Dr Patrick Delany, Dean of Down in Ireland: her first husband, to whom she was married off at the age of sixteen when he was over sixty (not a very happy arrangement), mercifully died seven years later.

Dr Delany, to whom she was happily espoused for twenty-five years, paid tribute to her as having "work for all hours and occasions, and finds full employment for her hands even between the coolings of her cups of tea!"

Her shellwork included the making of shell frames for drawings of the Duchess of Portland (Margaret Cavendish Bentinck, 1714–85), who was probably the largest collector of shells in Europe.

The Duchess, incidentally, introduced her to the Court at Windsor, where she became a firm favourite with the Royal Family. In 1785 George III gave her a house at Windsor, and a pension of £300 a year, which was personally placed in her hands every six months by Queen Charlotte "that it might escape the tax collector"!

Mrs Delany's shell cornice, made up of shell flowers, 86 large ones and 30 small ones, with which she decorated a room used as a chapel in her villa "Delville", near

41 SHELL AND SEAWEED PICTURE. Nineteenth century. A lavish border of tiny shells frames an elaborate, graceful composition of many-petalled flowers and delicate foliage all made up of shells and seaweed against a silk ground. *Mallett*

42 SHELL MOSAIC VALENTINE. Early nineteenth century. One half of an octagonal box featuring a Valentine made of shells, with a heart as a central motif. *City of Sheffield Museum*

43 SHELL MOSAIC VALENTINE. Early nineteenth century. The other half of an octagonal box featuring a Valentine made of shells, incorporating the loving message "Forget Me Not". *City of Sheffield Museum*

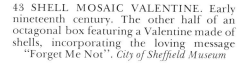

Dublin, survived until the middle 1900s when the house was pulled down and a hospital, Le Bon Secours, built in the grounds. Whether or not she made **shell pictures**, fashioned from shells and dried seaweed, we do not know. But, although rare, there are **shell nosegays** to be found, of eighteenth-century style, which might possibly have been made by her.

44 SHELL BASKET OF FLOWERS. Early nineteenth century. English. Some of the "blooms" are made up of at least twenty shells. *Victoria and Albert Museum*

45 SHELL ARCHWAY. Early nineteenth century. Ornate shell flowers are built up into an archway over a nautical scene. *Harris Museum and Art Gallery, Preston*

Mallett, of New Bond Street in London, specialize in searching out this decorative type of work and framing it superlatively, usually in a gilded box frame. They recently had a beautifully executed nosegay made entirely of shells. Jane Toller, in her book *Regency and Victorian Crafts*, suggests that it is not unreasonable to suppose that it might possibly be the work of the indefatigable Mrs Delany. Who knows? Anything as beautiful as this is worth collecting in its own right, whoever made it.

For seekers after shell pictures, there are some to be found. Some untouched, in their original frames, often maple or cork, others re-framed and with the shells possibly re-grouped and tidied if there has been some damage.

A fine example of a nineteenth-century shell-and-seaweed picture that I saw at Mallett's had an almost abstract quality; it had a lavish border of tiny, delicate shells framing the graceful composition of many-petalled flowers and foliage, all made up of shells and seaweed on a silk ground.

Some shell pictures were really **shell mosaic Valentines**. Obviously intended as love tokens, and probably made in the early 1800s, they are also referred to as "Sailor's Valentines". Whether they were actually made by seamen has not been established. Because so many of the boxes are similar in design, it is thought likely that they were made commercially, perhaps in the West Indies, for the men to take home to their sweethearts or wives.

34

The shell Valentines were two groupings of shells in octagonal wood frames, measuring about nine inches across, which were joined together by hinges, enabling them to be closed up as a box.

The box usually featured meticulously grouped sections of shells, with little clusters forming "roses", their petals made up of shells. In one half of the box would be a centre heart motif, in the other a loving platitude such as "Forget Me Not", the whole thing being covered in glass.

These shell mosaics are to be found on both sides of the Atlantic. The Chester Historical Society, West Chester, in the USA, has the complete hinged box with its shell message of "Truly Thine", similar to the one to be seen at Osborne House, Queen Victoria's holiday home in the Isle of Wight.

The City of Sheffield Museum in Britain has a shell nautical Valentine too, with the boxes unhinged and the "Forget Me Not" admonition.

The outlines of the design are formed in red and yellow cardboard, and then packed with brown paper and cottonwool to form a foundation for the shells.

Shells only are used to form the designs apart from the heart, which is made of small red beans. Most are British shells, but there are a few Mediterranean types. The Natural History Department of the Museum identified them as:

cockle (sometimes used broken into leaf-shaped fragments around the roses)
rough cockle
sea slug (Mediterranean)
tellins
limpets
cone or turret shell
oyster (?)
Venus
Netted dog whelk

They are all used in their natural colours except where the decoration is intended to resemble a rose and leaves when the tellins and cockles are tinted a bright pink and sea green. Some of the river-snail shells are also dyed a leaf-green colour.

Although these shell Valentines were never made for hanging on a wall, inevitably after the passage of time the hinges have got broken and the boxes separated; sometimes only one half of a box can be found. If you are lucky enough to find one, then obviously the wall is the place to display it.

Condition of the boxes will vary, according to whether the shells have become discoloured by dust getting in, or loosened and dislodged so that some are missing. One in extremely fine condition is the one in the Victoria and Albert Museum of c.1830, presented by the late Queen Mary.

An exquisite basket of flowers all made of shells was also presented to the Victoria and Albert by Queen Mary. Believed to be of early nineteenth-century origin, the floral arrangement is beautiful, with some of the "blooms" made up of over twenty shells which form the petals. The pot that they stand in is completely encrusted with

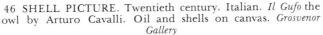

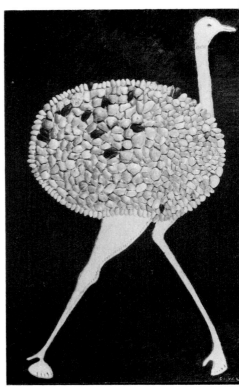

46 SHELL PICTURE. Twentieth century. Italian. *Il Gufo* the owl by Arturo Cavalli. Oil and shells on canvas. *Grosvenor Gallery*

47 SHELL PICTURE. Twentieth century. Italian. *Passo di Danza* by Arturo Cavalli. Oil and shells on canvas. *Grosvenor Gallery*

rows of tiny delicate shells. The exquisitely modelled flowers represent honeysuckle, lily-of-the-valley, passion flower, carnation, rose, anemones and others.

You can still find clusters of shells under glass domes. As a guide to what they look like, there are magnificent archways of shells made up almost completely of shell flowers, to be seen in the Philadelphia Museum of Art, the Victoria and Albert, and the Harris Museum and Art Gallery, Preston, Lancashire.

Victorian craft workers also embellished prints with frames of shells, and the popular periwinkles, winkles, mussels and pig-cowries would be stuck into wet plaster for frames for dressing-table mirrors and lids for trinket boxes. The natural, greyish outer scaling of the periwinkle would be removed with acetic acid to reveal the pearly iridescence beneath.

Godey's Lady Book in the 1840s, the leading American woman's magazine of its time, gave instructions for shellwork wreaths and bouquets to be hung in deep mahogany frames, or set under large glass bells. An early shell worker, who produced shell pictures, was Jane Loudon, 1807–63, and a woman better known as a landscape gardener and architect, Gertrude Jekyll, 1843–1932, also made beautiful shell pictures, I have seen one illustrated, signed 1928, which shows clusters of shells forming floral sprays.

Before we go back in time to other examples of shellwork, remember that modern shell pictures also exist for the collector, many of which can be classed as worthy heirlooms of the future.

48 SHELL PICTURE. Twentieth century. A contemporary shell picture made with shells from Welsh beaches. The shells are tinted, and "extras" to the picture include gold tipping on the white painted twigs, and pearl bead centres for the shell flowers. *Author's collection*

49 SHELL FIGURINE. 1760–1850. European or American. The figure is dressed in eighteenth-century costume made entirely of painted and lacquered shells—full bell-shaped skirt and apron, long sleeves, collar and cap. *The Henry Francis du Pont Winterthur Museum*

50 SHELL FIGURINE 1760–1850. The pair to 49. *The Henry Francis du Pont Winterthur Museum*

37

 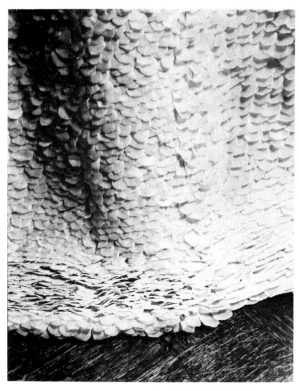

51 SHELL CURTAIN. Believed nineteenth century. An eight foot long curtain entirely made of shells. (The shell chair is painted silver and believed to be Regency.) *Ross Wills Collection*

52 SHELL CURTAIN (close-up). Note the enormous number of shells overlapping each other, all sewn on a silk backing.

In Italy Arturo Cavalli paints big birds in oil on canvas with dominant bodies filled in with large shells. *Il Gufo*, the owl, and *Passo di Danza*, a leggy ostrich dancing along, form part of a small collection of his work at London's Grosvenor Gallery.

Martha Ann Hodgson is an artist who loves the sea; the British wife of Patrick Hodgson, an American lawyer who is a conchologist, she makes beautiful shell flower arrangements. She never tints or paints the shells she uses, and they are often of the rare variety, gathered from the great shelling beaches of Florida, the Caribbean and the Far East.

Among the collectors of her work were Elizabeth the Queen Mother and politician Edward Heath. Her "signature" on a picture is a pair of wings, one of the lesser clams of a crustacean called sequila.

For her classical flower pieces she uses pale shells, white flushed with orange or pink, cream tinged with brown, all on a coloured felt ground. Large scallops and razor shells form the urns from which the flower patterns emerge. Her "submarine landscapes" have starfish and sea horses swimming through gardens of coral and pearl.

Another contemporary worker in shells is flower painter turned shell-artist Lady Gascoigne. Her compositions follow closely the graceful, traditional characteristics of Georgian shell work. One striking picture has an exquisite border using dozens of

53 SILHOUETTE. Eighteenth century. The Parminter family from à la Ronde, Exmouth going about their various leisure activities. By Torond. *Miss Tudor*

54 SHELL GALLERY. In à la Ronde, Exmouth, an eighteenth-century house in the round owned by the Parminter family. Shell panels alternate with feather work to give a mosaic effect. *Miss Tudor*

different limpet, spiral, cone and scallop shells, all tiny and delicate. It has a central bouquet of shell flowers flanked by shell birds.

If you look around seaside flower shops you can often find good, simple examples of modern shell pictures. One I have is the work of a woman in Llandudno, Wales. Her signature (she prefers to remain anonymous) is a sea-gull in the right-hand corner of her work, made up of two curved pieces of shell. She does touch up her pictures, gold-tipping the twigs of the stems of the shell flowers, and using pearl beads for the centre of the flowers. The result, a pleasant floral grouping of shells

55 SHELL HOUSE. Eighteenth century. English. In Goodwood House, Chichester, built by the second Duchess of Richmond and her daughters, it took seven years from 1739 to complete. A fabulous example of shellwork which completely covers the walls and ceiling.
The Trustees of the Goodwood Collection (Charles Howard)

40

in an oval of black felt edged with black braid, set against deep gold felt and the whole edged in black, is particularly striking.

Delightful shell figurines can be seen in the Shell Museum at Glandford in Norfolk, and there are also two in the Henry Francis du Pont Winterthur Museum in Delaware, USA.

These last two figurines, whose origin is uncertain (the Museum's catalogue card says probably serving wenches of the eighteenth century, their dates approximately 1760–1850, origin Europe or America), are approximately ten inches high, and represent the figure of a woman dressed in eighteenth-century costume made entirely of shells. The full, bell-shaped skirt, the long sleeves, wide collars, frilled bodice and head dress, are all composed of shells, many tiny, painted and lacquered. The shells are on a cloth backing, and the bust, hands and feet are of earthenware. (Some experts feel that the 1850 date is nearer the mark, as the costumes seem to be a Victorian interpretation rather than the real thing.)

The girls are holding platters of sea-food and shell-fish. These two doll-like characters have been preserved under a glass bell cover, which is why they are in such good condition. What is so fascinating about them is the way the shells have been worked to simulate both fabric and trimmings.

These dainty shell figures are rare (and expensive to buy), but they can be found. I saw two recently at a Brighton Antiques Fair. The pair were a man and woman, dressed in colourful shell outfits rather in the Spanish-peasant style.

Talking of Spain reminds me that down on their sunshine coasts is one place to look for shellwork when you are on holiday. Some of it is quite horrid, touristy stuff but I also saw some charming shell scenes of flowers, boats and figures mounted on highly varnished wood when I was on the Costa Blanca.

If you want to try your hand at making shell figures, Anthony Parker's *Shellcraft* gives simple instructions for making a crinoline lady. He uses four or five limpets for the skirt, a large tropical cowrie or small olive shell for the body, a small cowrie or Cornish winkle for the face, two horn shells for the arms, and glue and Barbola paste.

Two small cup shells are used for shoulder-pieces, a cockle for the bonnet, two small tellins to make a reticule, and a miniature limpet becomes a parasol.

For the model of an eighteenth-century figure he uses two mussels for a cloak, a whelk for a muff and a tellin for a hat.

A remarkable shell curiosity that a friend has is a pair of **shell curtains**. Yes, literally thousands of shells are sewn on a silk lining to form splendid-looking curtains over eight feet long by four feet wide.

The colour of the shells is a natural, rather dull white, and when they get dirty, as they obviously do in London's grime, they are just popped into the bath and washed!

If you want to observe shells *en masse* then take a look at the enchanting little Shell Museum, Glandford, Norfolk. The museum is full of shells collected over a period of sixty years by the late Sir Alfred Jodrell. They had been stored in boxes at Bayfield Hall until the museum was built in 1915.

Sir Alfred and his sisters Lady Seale and Mrs Ind arranged all the different shells in glass cases. The shells come from all over the world, and the collection is still being added to.

A **shell gallery** is a feature of a house called à la Ronde in Exmouth. The house was built in 1791 by two women, Jane and Mary Parminter, who after a holiday in Italy decided they wanted to have a round house on the same principle as the round church of San Vitale in Ravenna.

They decided to have the walls of the central gallery encrusted with mosaics, not of glass and stone, but of shells, seaweed and feathers, most of which were gathered from the Devonshire coast. Jane, incidentally, also made shell pictures, one of the Italian church she admired so much.

In the grounds of Goodwood House near Chichester in Sussex is a "Shell House", built by the second Duchess of Richmond and her daughters, Lady Caroline Fox and Emilie, Countess of Kildare. Their initials, with those of the Duke, are introduced into the decoration, which was started in 1739, and took seven years to complete.

Typical of the extraordinary yet quite magnificent shell grottoes of the eighteenth century, it was decorated with shells collected in the West Indies by Royal Navy officers. The interior of the pavilion is completely covered with shells on walls and ceiling; in alcoves are shell-encrusted vases full of shell flowers in sugar-icing colours of soft pink and mauve, interspersed with white.

Mary Delany, naturally, became involved in a spot of grotto-making. At Bulstrode in Buckinghamshire, scene of the Duchess of Portland's great collection (when it was auctioned in 1786 the sale comprised over four thousand separate lots), she helped to make a beautiful and elegant jewelled grotto in the garden, which included mother-of pearl, that nacreous lining of a pearl mussel.

The Duchess of Portland, referred to earlier in the chapter, was always active in adding to her collection of natural history. In 1774 Mary Delany refers to this warm-hearted pretty devotee as having returned from an expedition in Weymouth with this year's merchandise of sea plants and animals:

"She brought some extraordinary *vegetable animals* from the sea-side of the polypus kind, and she has had some three years that she keeps in basins of sea-water and they have increased since she had them. She has a green worm something like a centipede but of a much greater length . . . and a little red animal about the size and shape of a shrimp, that has four branches, which it puts out at pleasure, of a fine scarlet; and also throws out to a great length fine red strings with little roots at the end of each, so slender that you can but just discern them without a glass."

In Victorian times the art of shell-working was stepped up considerably, indus-trious-minded women making their way to the seashore to search for shells. Quite how they managed to cope with their elaborate dress when they foraged among sand and water must remain a mystery; and their outfits were far from simple.

In *The Ladies' Book of the Month*, September 1867, of which I have a tattered copy, Madame Elise, the editor, writing on "what a wondrous season this has been in the fashionable world", remarks that instead of styles getting more simple, "they are getting more extravagant and peculiar than ever. Short skirts are greatly in favour, and by the sea they look very picturesque." She illustrates two of these "seaside costumes"; the only thing short about them is that you can see the wearer's foot! She describes one as

> having petticoat of violet silk, bordered with black silk, edged with gold-coloured satin. Upper skirt and bodice of black silk, trimmed with gold-colour; sleeves of violet, trimmed with black silk and gold-coloured satin. Straw hat, trimmed with violet.

Shells could of course be bought commercially, done up in boxes and sold in shops, just as they can be today, so obviously some of the craft-workers had no need to get their feet wet.

In the USA "rice shells" – tiny specimens gathered in the West Indies – were particularly sought after. These were the basis of a very delicate art, which transformed them into jewellery, floral ornaments for the hair, and articles for the home such as card baskets and the like. A particularly exquisite floral cluster of these minute shells is in the Art Institute of Chicago.

At Arlington Court, Barnstaple, in Devon, built in 1820, there is an interesting collection of things from the sea, including model ships and shells. Arlington was the home of the Chichester family, who originated from Chichester in Sussex; the last Chichester to live in it was Rosalie Caroline Chichester (1865–1949), and on her death she bequeathed it to the National Trust. She had a large collection of British and foreign shells, which are displayed in cabinets in the house.

To the collection of model ships, which include a dozen of the "Little Ships" which rescued the British Army from Dunkirk in 1940, which Miss Chichester had specially reproduced, the National Trust have added a model of the Gipsy Moth IV in which Sir Francis Chichester completed his epic world voyage in 1967. Sir Francis' father was Rector of Shirwell, the parish next to Arlington. I have included this perhaps extraneous bit of information to show you when you start to turn over the stones of research, what interesting, and to me, anyway, absorbing, allied information you also come up with.

4

More From Sea and Garden

SEAWEED ALBUMS AND PICTURES
SAND PAINTINGS, BOTTLES AND BELLS
MOSS, BARK AND FERNS
LEAVES AND PRESSED FLOWERS

"Call us not weeds, we are flowers of the sea,
For lovely and bright and gay tinted are we,
And quite independent of sunshine or showers;
Then call us not weeds, we are ocean's gay flowers."

So went the trite traditional lines to be found on some **seaweed pictures**. Yet pressed and preserved seaweeds, with their lacy fronds pressed out like broad silk ribbons, some faded to a murky brown and various shades of sepia, can be quite attractive in an understated way.

Victorian women were just as keen on combing the beaches for seaweed as for shells, bundling it into buckets at low tide, to take home to lay on blotting paper to press between board or book.

When it was dry, they would either stick the specimens in a scrap book, or an album, or form it into a picture.

Victorian enthusiasts were guided by the book *A Popular History of Seaweeds* written by the Rev. Lansborough in 1849, and later a well-known writer of the period, a Mrs Gatty from Yorkshire (1809–73) wrote *British Seaweeds*, in which she included "Rules for the Preserving and Laying-out of Seaweeds".

Mrs Gatty, famed for *The Parables of Nature*, had taken up the study of seaweeds and, while working on her book, made a large number of seaweed albums which she sold for charity. Queen Victoria sent for one, remembering, no doubt, her own efforts at the age of fourteen when she had made a **seaweed album** while she was staying with her mother, the Duchess of Kent, in the Isle of Wight; she afterwards gave it to the little Queen of Portugal, Maria da Gloria, when she met her some while later.

What did a seaweed album look like? It was usually contained in two large scallop shells joined together with ribbon, into which leaves of paper were put to take the delicate strands of pressed seaweed.

They were quite intricate things to make, and in 1852 the *Lady's Newspaper* referred to "a fanciful and very elaborate book, the binding of which is composed of two large fan-formed shells, enclosing leaves whereon seaweed is secured".

44

56 SHELL PICTURE. Twentieth century. Contemporary shell arrangement by Martha Hodgson.

57 SHELL PICTURE. Twentieth century. Contemporary shell picture by Martha Hodgson.

58 SEAWEED PICTURE. Early nineteenth century. Various dried seaweeds made to form a floral arrangement in a small wicker basket, mounted on hand-made paper and reframed in a modern gilt frame. *Mallett*

I have seen several seaweed pictures, which are mainly fronds of various seaweeds arranged in a small basket. The whole is mounted on paper and then framed in a box frame under glass. They are not very colourful, so I think you have to decide if they are worth having for their curiosity value, and the fact that they have survived all this time.

A delightful collage picture in seaweed and sand was worked by the Parminter family of à la Ronde, Exmouth, whom I mentioned earlier. Strips of seaweed are used for tree trunks, seaweed for the foliage, and sand for the driveway leading to a house.

Artistry in **sand** was a strange and attractive art which developed in this country in the late eighteenth and nineteenth centuries through the work of some talented immigrant confectioners employed at the court of George III.

These men were "table-deckers" who made marvellous decorations for the festive table. These arrangements were made from materials such as coloured sugar, pow-

59 SEAWEED AND SAND COLLAGE. Late eighteenth century. English. The Avenue, made by Jane Parminter. It is a watercolour of an eighteenth-century house with an avenue of seaweed trees and a sandy drive. *Miss Tudor*

60 SAND PAINTING. Probably late eighteenth century. Believed to be by Zobel after a painting by George Morland. *Pamela Davies at National Collectors' Fair*

dered glass, marble dust and, eventually, coloured sands. All these were laid out in a design on a cloth, tray or board, and after the party was over, swept away.

One of the table-deckers was Benjamin Zobel, who was born in Memmingen, Germany, in 1762, and who, although trained as a confectioner, also studied portrait painting in Amsterdam before going to London at the age of twenty-one. Installed at Court at Windsor, he became so keen on these sand creations, known as the art of "marmotinto", that he discovered an adhesive whereby he could make them permanent; this, it is said, at the direct request of George III, who was delighted with his work.

Zobel made his pictures by first drawing a design or scene on a piece of stout millboard, and then, section by section, it was treated with an adhesive substance (no one was quite sure what this was, as the work was carried out in the utmost secrecy, behind locked doors), on which the appropriate coloured sand or marble dust was carefully scattered.

When this had dried, another part of the composition was started, and so the picture gradually took shape. The whole operation was very tricky, and required great skill, because obviously sand is difficult stuff to fix permanently on to board. The artist had to be capable of doing the initial drawing, and handling the sands, controlling their flow so as to cover one exact spot on a small surface.

The subjects he chose for his sand paintings – Windsor Castle, battle scenes, biblical subjects, animals, etc. were various, and were often copies of pictures already painted by other artists – George Morland, Benjamin West, George Stubbs, Abraham Cooper and others. In general they were dark, gloomy vistas of stags and mountain sheep in shadows and dim twilight. I saw two of them at a Grosvenor House Antiques Fair, so they are still to be found.

Some of Zobel's work is signed, and one landscape I have seen had written on the back "designed by Morland for B. Zobel while in the Isle of Wight 1793", so he must have met Morland when they were both staying on the Isle of Wight. A painting in sand of a brewer's dray and horses is believed to be by Zobel after Morland.

Zobel had eight children, and one of these, James, also did beautiful and arresting sand paintings. He lived and worked in Norwich after a brief spell at the table-decking job. He specialized in sand portraits of horses and dogs – a white horse in sand is quite something.

Another German, George Lewis Haas, also did sand paintings, but in lighter, more glaring, jewel-like colours. Some of his rural scenes had raised foliage, whereas Zobel's pictures were much flatter.

It is said that the two had different methods of fixing their pictures. Zobel spiralled his sand into a sticky board, whereas Haas fixed his designs after by spraying on a secret gum-like formula.

There is a record of at least one public exhibition of Haas's work, which included a self-portrait (a rare item), Welsh landscapes and animal studies.

Another sand painter, from Holland this time, was Frederick Schweikhardt. His father, W. J. Schweikhardt, came over from Holland during the troubles of 1786, and frequently exhibited at the Royal Academy.

61 SAND PICTURE. Osborne House, Isle of Wight, holiday home of Prince Albert and Queen Victoria. Probably after 1848 when the second tower was completed. Unsigned. *Author's collection*

Frederick, unlike the others, often overpainted his sand pictures with water colours, so successfully combining two methods of artistry. He painted several large flower pictures after Van Huysen.

After this coterie of overseas artists departed from the scene, there was a long gap in the art of marmotinto until about 1840, when a new and simpler type of sand picture emerged from a group of Isle of Wight artists.

They were much smaller in size than the earlier efforts, and were made from the unusual coloured sands of Alum Bay which ranged from pale yellow to gold, dark green to olive. Three artists' names that have emerged are Edwin Dore and J. Neat of Newport, both working about 1836 to 1840, and, much later, about 1910, R. J. Snow of Lake, near Sandown.

Most of the work featured local beauty spots and historical buildings, such as Carisbrooke Castle, Ventnor, Whippingham and Arreton churches, and, of course, Osborne House, Prince Albert and Queen Victoria's holiday home on the Isle of Wight, completed about 1848. I have one of Osborne plus a collection of Edwin Dore's tiny sand pictures, all signed and dated in his precise, neat hand, inscribed "drawn with Alum Bay sand". They were found in a sketch book in Brighton.

If you want to try your hand at sand pictures, you can buy the coloured sands of the area in little packets at Alum Bay. There are modern sand pictures for sale there, but I am afraid they are rather crude and don't compare with the delicacy of the period work.

A form of sand painting was known as a home craft in the United States. Frances Lichten in *Decorative Art of Victoria's Era* describes how:

49

Vari-coloured sands were first collected. Then, after a painting had been blocked out very simply in water colour, sand in colours vaguely approximating the desired hues was carefully sifted over selected areas previously coated with mucilage. Details in the painting were brought out with accents of powdered colour mixed with glue.

Miss Lichten also refers to marble dust painting:

This was a process by which a gloomy landscape drawing was evolved in black pastel on a ground which had been coated with glue over which marble dust had been sifted and left to dry before using.

I have heard of beautiful **sand bottles** made in Mississippi by an Andrew Clemens, around 1889, some of which are in the Iowa State Historical Museum. Inside an ordinary mid-Victorian round-top bottle he built up pictures in the sand, grain by grain, of George Washington, the Mississippi river boats, and ocean sailing vessels.

What was probably a similar idea, although much cruder, were the British **sand bells**. These were bell-shaped glasses filled with layers of different coloured sands, part of which were formed into views of the Needles Rock or Shanklin Chine.

Both these last sand curiosities would take a bit of searching for. Glass is fragile, and once it is broken, the picture inside would pour away.

But sand paintings and pictures can be found. Recent writers have called attention to their under-valuation, which means, I am afraid, prices have started to rise.

Other piquant curiosities of the mid-Victorian era were pictures trimmed with **moss** and **bark**. Sea- and landscapes in which a ruin would be prominent would have the painted walls of the ruin adorned with bark painted white; any rocks in the foreground would have bits of moss glued to them. Realism was all in these artistic-botanical mélanges!

Sometimes the moss (a woodland, or even a seaside treasure, for what else is it but a low, tufted herbaceous plant usually growing on damp soil, stones or trees?) would be used as a frame for a picture, after being dried and bleached and sometimes dyed.

Moss would even become the major part of a picture; the Red House Museum in Christchurch has a confection made of wool flowers, and presumably worked over wire, and the industrious worker's name, Emma Kemp, placed in the centre of a bed of moss.

Moss leads quite naturally to **leaves** and **flowers**. Autumn leaves were highly thought of as decorative items in the mid 1800s. In 1851 some New England women sent from America, to the Great Exhibition in London, an ornamental arrangement of autumn leaves, as their artistic contribution from their respective States.

Making **skeleton leaves** was a popular pastime too. The method for producing these phantom bouquets is of course to be found in the ubiquitous *Enquire Within Upon Everything*:

The leaves should be put into an earthen or glass vessel, and a large quantity of rain water poured over them; after this they must be left in the open air, and to the heat of the sun, without covering the vessel. As the water evaporates

62 SAND PICTURE. Nineteenth century. English. Carisbrooke Castle, Isle of Wight, drawn with Alum Bay sand by Edwin Dore. *Pamela Davies. Author's collection*

63 SAND PICTURE. Nineteenth century. English. Arched Rock, Freshwater Bay, Isle of Wight, drawn with Alum Bay sand by Edwin Dore. Signed and dated 1838. *Pamela Davies. Author's collection*

51

64 SKELETON LEAF PICTURE. *c.* 1840. Imposing grouping of dried-skeleton leaves, flowers and seaweed, mounted on a modern green craquelure background, and framed in a deep gold box frame. *Mallett*

and the leaves become dry, more water must be added; the leaves will by this means putrefy, but the time required for this varies; some plants will be finished in a month, others will require two months or longer, according to the toughness of their parenchyma.

When they have been in a state of putrefaction for some time, the two membranes will begin to separate, and the green part of the leaf to become fluid; then the operation of clearing is to be performed. The leaf is to be put upon a flat white earthen plate, and covered with clear water; and being gently squeezed with the finger, the membranes will begin to open, and the green substance will come out at the edges; the membranes must be carefully taken off with the finger, and great caution must be used in separating them near the middle rib. When once there is an opening towards this separation, the whole membrane follows easily; when both membranes are taken off, the skeleton is finished, and it has to be washed clean with water, and then dried between the leaves of a book.

A fancywork novelty concerned with foliage which caught on in the United States was **spatter-work**. The technique was applied to pictures, lampshades, curtains and screens.

To carry out the "spattering" you fastened down various pressed ferns and leaves with pins on to light-coloured paper, wood or fabric, arranging them in a graceful composition first. You then sprayed the lot with a fine spray of Indian ink, spattered from a toothbrush through a wire sieve. On taking away the leaves and so on, you were left with a well-defined silhouette on a shaded ground – a delicately attractive novelty.

The Chester County Historical Society in West Chester, USA, have a spatter-work wall decoration.

Taking **leaf impressions** was in fashion at the turn of the nineteenth century, and here again the ever-present *Enquire Within* gives an intriguing method:

52

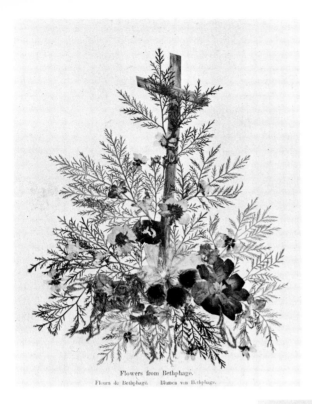

Flowers from Bethphage.
Fleurs de Bethphage.   Blumen von Bethphage.

65 PRESSED FLOWER PICTURE. *c. 1875.* Taken from a book from the Holy Land. The book has an olive wood cover typical of many albums of the period. *The Bowes Museum, Barnard Castle*

66 PRESSED FLOWER PICTURE. *c. 1875.* Taken from a book from the Holy Land. The book has an olive wood cover typical of many albums of the period. *The Bowes Museum, Barnard Castle*

Flowers from Haceldama.
Fleurs d'Haceldama.   Blumen von Haceldama.

67 PRESSED FLOWER PICTURE. Twentieth century. A contemporary flower picture by Pamela McDowall, using clematis, Iceland poppies, silver leaf and raspberry and blackberry leaves. *Pressed Flower Pictures* by Pamela McDowall

68 PRESSED FLOWER PICTURE. Twentieth century. A contemporary flower picture by Pamela McDowall, using yellow daisies, clematis and raspberry and blackberry leaves. *Pressed Flower Pictures* by Pamela McDowall

Hold oiled paper in the smoke of a lamp or of pitch, until it becomes coated with the smoke; to this paper apply the leaf of which you wish to make an impression, having previously warmed it between your hands, that it may be pliable. Place the lower surface of the leaf upon the blackened surface of the oil-paper, that the numerous veins, which are so prominent on this side, may receive from the paper a portion of the smoke. Lay a paper over the leaf, and then press it gently upon the smoked paper with the fingers, or with a small roller covered with woollen cloth, or some similarly soft material, so that every part of the leaf may come in contact with the sooted oil-paper. A coating of the smoke will adhere to the leaf. Then remove the leaf carefully, and place the blackened surface on a sheet of white paper, or in a book prepared for the purpose, covering the leaf with a clean slip of paper, and pressing upon it with the fingers, or roller, as before. With care excellent impressions may be thus obtained.

As part of the consuming interest in botany during the eighteenth and nineteenth centuries, obviously collecting wild flowers for pressing and preserving in albums was a favourite pastime. You are quite likely to find some of these sentimental souvenirs flattened between the pages of Victorian novels – faded, formless blossoms placed there as loving reminders of a romance long gone.

Just coming into fashion as modest collector's pieces are those **pressed flowers** from the Holy Land, so common as souvenirs in the 1870s to 1890s. They can often be found in scrapbooks of the period, or in small albums with an olive wood cover,

69 MATCHBOXES DECORATED WITH PRESSED FLOWERS AND LEAVES. Twentieth century. English. The one on the left is decorated with mimosa and montbretia. The other design is made out of various petals and the leaves of the meadow buttercup. *Pressed Flower Collages* by Pamela McDowall

70 PRESSED FLOWERS IN PLASTIC. Twentieth century. English. Flowers encased in transparent plastic make pretty modern paperweights. *Pressed Flower Collages* by Pamela McDowall

honey-coloured and shiny. The Bowes Museum, Barnard Castle, Co. Durham, have recently included two examples in their collection of Victorian work. Described as Fleurs de Bethphagé and Fleurs d'Haceldama, the colours of the flowers and ferns are still fresh and bright.

Pamela McDowall in her *Pressed Flower Pictures – A Victorian Art Revived* illustrates two cards of pressed flowers found in an 1880 scrapbook. One, dated 1883, shows Mary at the Holy Sepulchre; the other (1889) is from Jaffa, sending a Christmas greeting to England in Arabic. In both, the delphiniums are still blue.

If you want to indulge in this nostalgic art yourself then read this book and the follow-up, *Pressed Flower Collages*, which is full of clear how-to-do-it pictures. In her work Pamela McDowall uses flowers, ferns and leaves; maple, chestnut, aspen, poplar and oak leaves are all pressed when the leaves are very tender and have an almost translucent appearance of greeny-yellow and pink. Her style is to keep every petal, stem and leaf separate from the next so that all is shown off to its best advantage, vastly different from the Victorian clutter. She presses the leaves with everything from an old trouser press to an iron set at the heat mark for "wool"!

5

Pictures with Felt, Fabric and Tinsel

THE DUKE AND THE LADY
FELT, FLANNEL AND FABRIC PICTURES
RIBBON AND PATCH
DRESSED PRINTS AND TINSEL PORTRAITS
CONTEMPORARY COLLAGE

*"It is not that artistic power has left the world, but that a more rapid
life has developed itself in it, leaving no time for deliberate dainty decoration, or labours of love."*

The Drawing Room – Its Decorations and Furniture 1877
MRS ORRINSMITH

He beams like a cherub, in spite of his whiskers. She sits serenely in a garden chair at
his side. He is believed to be the Duke of Sussex (1773–1843), sixth son of George III
and Queen Charlotte, but who is she?

The lady and the Duke are figures in a stitched **felt picture** that I have, which
has him in the sombre black robes of a friar. If you take a look at some pencil and
chalk sketches of the Duke done around 1832, you will see that the painted paper
face which is stuck above the holy garb is undoubtedly that of Augustus Frederick,
raised to the peerage as Baron Arklow, Earl of Inverness and Duke of Sussex in
1801, strong supporter of the progressive political party, Grand Master of Freemasons
and one-time president of both the Society of Arts and the Royal Society.

But whether his companion is his wife, Lady Angela Murray, whom he married
in 1793, is a moot point, because the marriage was promptly declared void under
the Royal Marriage Act, 1794. But the picture is a collector's gem, something that
is just a little bit different, and it always makes a good talking point!

The date is probably late Regency, 1830s, because the Duke died when he was
seventy in 1843, and he would have been late fifties or so in the felt picture. Actually
he had lost a lot of hair since the canvas of him done in 1798 by G. Head, which
is in the National Portrait Gallery. In it his curly locks fall beyond his collar and go kiss-
curl fashion on his cheek.

Other favourite felt confections of the period, with much more cut-work involved,
were those featuring a basket of strawberries, easily life-size or larger. At a recent
Grosvenor House Antiques Fair I saw two such fruit baskets. One was an extremely

56

71 FELT PICTURE. Early nineteenth century. English. The figure of the man is believed to be the Duke of Sussex (1773–1843); but who is the lady? *E. Tudor-Hart. Author's collection*

large work, and before I had time to note the exact details was whisked away by a buyer at a figure exceeding £200! (480.00 dollars). The other, at a much more modest sum, was smaller, in what would have been its original Sheraton gilded box frame, probably *c*. 1795. Set in an oval against a dark ground, the weaving of the long, cone-shaped basket was most realistic, and the strawberries, rich and red looking, with their flecked markings stitched on in lighter shade, extremely appetizing.

These works are rare, and in their original frames obviously costly. More available are available are felt flower pictures, although they do take some searching out. Beautifully grouped flower sprays could include passion flowers, auriculas, rose buds and some foliage. One such bouquet I have seen is believed to have been worked by Mrs Fitzherbert, mistress of the Prince Regent, later George IV;

A flower and fruit picture dating from the end of the eighteenth century, worked "in an application of pieces of cloth on a ground of dull white flannel", is referred to by Gertrude Jekyll in her book *Old West Surrey*, published in 1904. In a chapter on cottage ornaments she illustrates a picture in appliqué and embroidery of a basket of flowers surrounded by strawberries.

The flower is the auricula, strikingly lifelike, in two shades of brown over white; the "antlers", in their natural straw-colours, being knots of silk. Wrote Mrs Jekyll:

The spray of pansy is of white and purple cloth, pencilled with fine slate-

57

72 PENCIL AND CHALK SKETCHES OF THE DUKE OF SUSSEX. *c.* 1832 by F. Chantrey.
He looks rather like the man in the felt picture, doesn't he? *National Portrait Gallery*

73 PORTRAIT DUKE OF
SUSSEX. 1798. Painted by G. Head
when the Duke was about 25 before
he lost his hair. *National Portrait
Gallery*

74 FELT FRUIT BASKET. *c.* 1795. English. The strawberries are in rich red felt with stitched markings, the basket in natural coloured strips of felt. In original Sheraton gilt box frame. *Ronald Phillips*

75 FELT FLOWER PICTURE. Early nineteenth century. English. A spray of flowers cut in felt with some surface needlework thought to have been done by Mrs Fitzherbert, mistress of the Regent George IV. *Filkins*

76 FELT FLOWER PICTURE. Late eighteenth century. A basket of flowers in felt mounted on a modern stone-coloured craquelure background, and framed in gilt. *Mallett*

77 FELT APPLIQUÉD CUSHION COVER. *c.* 1850.
Flowers and motifs are of coloured felt on a velvet ground.
Victoria and Albert Museum

78 RIBBON PICTURE. Believed Victorian. A cottage scene with bands of ribbon forming the wood slats of the wall, frames of the window, and thatch of the roof. Aerophane (coloured silk gauze) is used for flowers and foliage. *Private collection*

coloured corded silk. The tiger-lilies, very small in scale, are of orange plush. The leaves of the rose are of pale green cloth, heavily worked over with very fine worsted crewel of nearly the same colour; the petal part of the rose and buds are of floss silk.

"The basket is of buff cloth, the pattern perforated. The strawberries are also very near nature; they are not merely cut out, but the edges are turned back, giving each fruit a distinct projection." Truly a labour of love!

In London's Bethnal Green Museum there is a rich-looking cushion cover *c.* 1850, made of coloured felt flowers and motifs, appliquéd on to a velvet ground, embroidered over in coloured silks. There must be many of these around for the collector, although you have to be prepared for a spot of moth, felt being a favourite food for these hide-away creatures.

Numerous dainty decorations were painstakingly made up of fabrics of all kinds. Complete pictures were often built up with **ribbon** and pieces of brightly coloured silk gauze known as **aerophane**. A friend has a charming cottage scene with bands of ribbon forming the wood slats of the wall, frames of windows, thatch of the roof and the stack of the chimney, surrounded by gauzy foliage, flowers and trees, and a chicken on a painted path. This is the only one I have seen like this (purchased for next to nothing in a junk yard!), but there must be others around for the diligent collector.

A remarkable collection of **patchwork pictures** was made by Mrs R. H. Harris of

79 PATCHWORK PICTURE. Late nineteenth century. English. A christening scene at Christmas by Mrs R. H. Harris, all worked in tiny patches. It is signed and dated 1876 in the lower left-hand corner. On display at the *Royal Shakespeare Theatre, Stratford-upon-Avon*

80 PATCHWORK PICTURE. Late nineteenth century. William Glover's Shop by Mrs R. H. Harris, all in minute patches, except for the curtains at the window which are in aerophane. *Royal Shakespeare Theatre, Stratford-upon-Avon*

Stratford-upon-Avon in the latter half of the nineteenth century. You can see them in the foyer of the Royal Shakespeare Theatre in Stratford. One of them is a delightful Christmas christening scene, signed and dated "R. Harris 1876"; the clothes of all the tiny figures are made up of pieces of the appropriate material, such as broderie anglaise for the baby's christening robe. Another of her patchwork pictures features a view of William Glover's shop, all worked in minute patches, with the exception of the curtains which are in that gauzy aerophane.

Other patchwork pictures were made more recently by Miss Elizabeth Allen, who was discovered and publicized as England's Grandma Moses. Her pictures, which belong to the category of "primitive" works, were exhibited at the Crane Kalman Gallery when she was eighty-two. Her ideas were fantasies of the East mixed in with the Arabian Nights fairy tales and her own strong sense of morality.

Her pictures have a singularly period appearance, although many were made in this century. She used faded silks, shredded satins, worn suede, flannel, pieces of patterned fabric, beads and sequins, using blanket and chain stitches to outline some of the patches. In "Babylon Riding the Great Dragon", thick lace is used to great effect; in "The Great Pyramid" she used coloured sequins to make a glittering crown.

"Dressed" prints make an unusual item for the collector. Figures in print were

61

81 DRESSED PRINT. Early nineteenth century. French. A print from the *Journal des Demoiselles* "dressed" in bright fabrics. *R. B. Dickson*

82 DRESSED PRINT. *c.* 1840. English. Two unidentified women at Midgham House, the family seat of W. S. Poyntz Esq, M.P. *Starting Fabric Collage. Frances Kay*

padded and "dressed" with actual fragments of material for the garments to represent real clothes. Sometimes the gowns to be dressed were ornamented with tiny pieces of precious stones, seed pearls, or minute bits of coloured glass.

These dressed prints were also called "Amelias", as it is thought that Amelia Blackburn, the invalid lady of the early 1800s, who was so skilful with her cut-paper work, initiated the idea.

It required a great deal of patience and skill to manipulate such tiny pieces of fabric and ornament, and one dressed print from the *Journal des Demoiselles*, featuring two smart women of fashion, incorporates fancy lace trimming on the tiers of one woman's dress and fabric cleverly ruched-up to form a crinoline on her companion.

Another effective dressed print I have seen, dating from about 1840, shows a water-colour print of Midgham House, the family seat of one W. A. Poyntz, Esq., M.P. (or anyway so the inscription on the back goes). The view of the house has a surround of shells stuck on to a cord-edged card, giving the appearance of a shell grotto. Looking through the archway of shells are two females clothed in muslins and be-ribboned bonnets, complete with reticules and paper dogs, a pug and poodle.

In the 1830s to 1850s the craze was for buying prints of popular actors and actresses and royal personages in exaggerated stance, with one knee bent and one leg straight, the figure lunging forwards like a fencer completing a thrust. Sometimes the pictures were bought ornamented, or packets of shapes in various satin and feathers, and tiny bits of fabric, silk, and glinting, glowing coloured tinsels could be bought separately to decorate them.

83 SAND PICTURE. Nineteenth century. English. Ventnor Church when the church was built in 1837. Unsigned. *Red House Museum, Christchurch*

84 ALUM BAY, ISLE OF WIGHT. Contemporary. The coloured sand of the area on sale in the Alum Bay kiosk, with a group of period sand pictures in the background. *Trevor Kenyon*

85 WOOL AND MOSS PICTURE. The petalled flowers and the name Emma Kemp are worked in wool over wire, and set in a bed of moss. *Red House Museum, Christchurch*

86 TINSEL PRINT. Nineteenth century. English. Madame Vestris, a popular actress in the mid-1800s, as Don Giovanni. The print is dressed up with bits of coloured fabric and tinsel. Maple frame. *Arundel Antiques Market. Author's Collection*

87 COLLAGE. Contemporary fabric picture by Frances Kay of Queen Elizabeth I. Rich velvet, lace, pearls, bead and braid have been used for the colourful costume. *Starting Fabric Collage*

Mr Elton as Richard Coeur de Lion could be given realistic-looking armour and jewelled sword, while other characters could be ornamented with coloured metal foil, plumes, rosettes, stars, spangles and warlike daggers embossed and backed with paper.

I have a **tinsel print** in its original maple frame of Madame Vestris, a popular actress of the mid 1800s, in the role of Don Giovanni, she being a lady who specialized in taking men's roles. Her impressive garb includes a lavishly decorated blue tunic with red-fringed sash, silver tights, gold tinsel slippers, jewelled bracelets at arm and ankle, and large be-plumed hat.

Currently there are many artists making novel and interesting **fabric collage** pictures, incorporating a variety of rich fabrics, with many owing their inspiration to the decorative fancies of our ancestors.

Frances Kay in *Starting Fabric Collage* points out that the word collage comes from the French verb *coller*, to paste or glue. "You can stretch the term to cover a picture in which some stitching is used to decorate or reinforce the fabrics, but if the picture is mainly put together with needle and thread, then it isn't fabric collage, it's embroidery."

In her book she shows a selection of pictures made from beads, braids, ribbons, felt, gauzes, lace, net, string; most striking is her fabric picture of Queen Elizabeth I in a gown of velvet trimmed with laces, pearls, beads and braid.

88 COLLAGE. Contemporary fabric picture by
Charles Hammick of a Field Officer (staff) Welsh
Guards in present day Guard of Honour order.
Starting Fabric Collage. Frances Kay

89 COLLAGE. 1960. E. L. T. Mesens. "Parmi Les Palais, Les Statues . . ." of
coloured foil and various papers. *Grosvenor Gallery*

90 COLLAGE. 1955. Enrico Baj.
Coloured glass and oil. *Grosvenor
Gallery*

91 COLLAGE. Contemporary. Enrico Baj. "Enfant aux Miroirs" in mirror and paint on brocade. *Grosvenor Gallery*

65

Charles Hammick, an ex-Guards officer, specializes in fabric pictures of field officers, all correct in every detail of buttons, braids, cords and decorations. Eugenie Alexander, Christine Risley, Eirian Short, Margaret Kaye, Beldy – all are now famous in the world of contemporary collage. Beldy, daughter of animal painter Heyward Hardy, believes that if all ideas of needlework and decoration conceptions were put aside, and materials properly used and blended in a painting fashion, they could give results every bit as interesting as water colour, oil, or gouache.

E. E. T. Mesens (1903–71) used coloured foil and papers for his distinctive collages; while Enrico Baj (born in Milan in 1924), uses all sorts of odd things in his work, which covers collages, assemblages and paintings. "All material already used by life" is how one writer describes them – mattress covers, wallpapers, medals, cords, buttons and bows!

His "Lady Sensitive to the Weather", which won the Zika Ascher award in 1966 for the best work of art utilizing fabrics in collage, was made up of thick cloth-braids, beads, jewelled eyes and a thermometer in the centre of the face! Another rather odd "lady" was created out of fabric, coloured glass and oil, while yet another figure, Enfant aux Miroirs", was formed of a mosaic of bits and coloured glass against a brocade background. All these works are at the Grosvenor Gallery in London.

I started off this chapter with simple stitched felt pictures. I have finished it in the fantasy realms of contemporary collage. Collectors will make their own choice of what pictures they will include in their collection, remembering of course that works of art can be created from almost any material – consider the brilliant news-paper collages of Picasso and the wood strips of Braque's still-lifes.

66

6

Other Decorative Fancies

DECALCOMANIE AND POTICHIMANIE
PAINTING ON VELVET – STENCILS AND THEOREMS
PAINTING ON GLASS AND RIBBON

"Nothing sooner becomes obsolete than a fashionable amusement."

The Girl's Home Companion, edited Mrs Valentine, early twentieth century

There are hundreds of examples of home handicrafts of less than a century ago lurking hidden away, for enterprising collectors to cast their eyes on. Hobbies that flourished like mad when they were in vogue, but which completely faded from the scene as the next fashionable occupation took their place.

The Victorians had crazes for things – manias, you might say. One of them, back in the 1840s, was for **decalcomanie**, literally derived from the French *décalquage* or *décalque*, leaving counter tracing or transfer, and of course, *manie*, a mania or craze.

The Lady's Book of the Month (1867) advertised it as "Decalcomanie, The New and Beautiful Art of Transferring Instantly Pictures to China, Glass, Wood, Silk and Other Materials". Complete boxes of the materials were not cheap by Victorian standards either, some were more than £2 ($4.80), although books of instructions, with lists of designs and materials could be had for a modest sum.

I can offer you the complete method of making the objects of this particular craze from the *Enquire Within* 1872 version.

First of all decalcomanie was described as "this recently discovered beautiful art consisting of transferring coloured drawings to glass, porcelain, china, wood, silver, furniture, plaster-of-Paris, alabaster, ivory, paper, paper hangings" . . . the list is endless. Almost anything of any shape or size, provided it had a smooth surface. "The immediate result being an exact resemblance to painting by hand." What more could you ask?

The materials required were:
1. A bottle of transfer varnish for fixing the drawing.
2. A bottle of light varnish to pass over the drawing when fixed.
3. A bottle of spirit to clean brushes and to remove those pictures which did not come out right.
4. A piece of beaver cloth about nine inches square.
5. A paper knife and roller.

92 DECALCOMANIE. Advertisement from *The Lady's Book of the Month,* 1867

93 POTICHIMANIE.
Mid-1800s. French. Parlour craft whereby a plain glass or porcelain vase or jar (*potiche*), was decorated with scraps of brightly coloured designs pasted on the *inside* of the transparent glass. The whole was then varnished over to keep it in place.

94 DIAPHANIE. Advertisement from *The Lady's Book of the Month,* 1867

6. Two or three camel hair brushes.
7. A basin of water.
8. A bottle of opaque varnish.

Instructions

Thoroughly clean and free from grease the article to be decorated; then cut off the white paper margin of the drawing, dipping one of the brushes into the transfer varnish and giving it a very light coat, being especially careful to

95 PAINTING ON VELVET.
Early nineteenth century.
American. Fruit in a basket painted
in bright colours on white cotton
velvet.

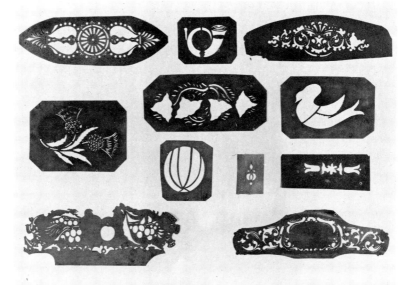

96 STENCILS. First half
nineteenth century.
American. Group of
paper stencils from a
collection used in
Tynsboro, Massachusetts.
*The Smithsonian Institute,
Washington DC*

cover the whole of the coloured portion but not to allow it to touch the blank paper. Then lay the drawing, face downward, on the object to be ornamented taking care to place it only where it is to remain, as it would be spoilt by moving. If the varnish on its first application is too liquid, allow the picture to remain for ten minutes to set.

Moisten the cloth with water, and lay it gently on the drawing which is being previously laid in its place, on the object to be decorated. Then rub it over with the paper knife or roller so as to cause the print to adhere to every part; this done, remove the cloth, well soak the paper with a camel hair brush dipped in water and immediately after lift the paper by one corner and lift and gently draw it off.

The picture will be left on the object while the paper will come off perfectly white. Care must be taken that the piece of cloth without being too wet is sufficiently so to saturate the paper completely. The drawing must now be washed with a camel hair brush in clean water to remove the surplus varnish and then left till quite dry. On the following day cover the picture with a light coat of the fixing varnish to give brilliance to the colour.

Next mania coming up is **potichimanie** – *potiche* in French meaning glass or porcelain vase or jar.

Potichimanie was a parlour craft whereby a plain glass vase or jar was effectively decorated with scraps of brightly coloured designs and drawings pasted on the *inside* of the transparent glass, which was then varnished over to keep them in position. Its maker could then fondly imagine the vase as the equal of any Dresden, Sèvres or Chinese porcelain!

In a woman's journal of 1873 the heroine, Lady Jane, wrote: "I should advise 'Marquise de Conflans' to make a potichimanie vase with her scraps; if grounded in pale blue or pink, it might be made to look like a Sèvres vase."

The "art", if you can call it that, was popular in the United States where sheets of paper printed in colours with motifs appropriate to the different styles could be bought, and indeed featured Dresden medallions, Etruscan designs and Chinese figures and flowers. The ground in between the scraps of glued-on paper was filled in with oil colours.

A candlestick in Mrs Pullan's *Lady's Manual of Fancy Work* (1859) has borders of grapes, leaves and medallions of French buildings in deep blue and gold.

John Bedford in his *Still Looking for Junk* wrote of "some handsome examples which often turn up at sales, their colours still bright under their glass skin".

Potichimanie in America finally deteriorated in the 1880s to the pasting of coloured figures to the *outside* of ordinary pottery jars, which were called "Dolly Varden" jars. The whole thing had a final fling at the turn of the century when gold and embossed cigar bands were glued to the under surface of glass trays as well as jugs. Rather awful, but as Katherine Morrison McClinton remarks in *Antique Collecting For Everyone*: "Who knows, we may be collecting these jugs for the names of cigars no longer made!"

We have not quite finished with our crazes yet though. There was **vitre manie**, where decorative patterns were transferred on window glass by a simple process (cf. *vitre*, pane of glass, *vitrail*, stained-glass window). This was presumably similar to *diaphanie*, which was referred to in the 1867 *Lady's Book of the Month* as "bearing a close resemblance to the costly stained glass of the old process . . . applicable to windows of all kinds – church, staircase, conservatory etc.".

It was obviously practised as a trade rather than a home craft (although I expect the do-it-yourselfers had a go), and you can still see a bit of it about in old houses, usually on the glass lobby door just inside the main front door.

Painting on velvet was another decorative fancy of the 1800s. It was first achieved

97 POONAH PAINTING. Damask Rose design for painting on velvet. English. *The Young Ladies' Journal Complete Guide to the Work-Table, 1885*

DIAGRAM OF COLOURED DESIGN FOR DAMASK ROSE.

DIRECTIONS FOR POONAH PAINTING ON VELVET, SATIN. SILK. &c.
    To make the directions for Poonah Painting as useful and practical as possible, we have prepared a Damask Rose and Foliage in Colours, as being a simple design for a beginner to practise with. The diagrams for formulas for the rose will also give a correct idea of preparing a more complicated design, such as a group of flowers like our June Roses, &c.

98 POONAH PAINTING. Diagram of "Coloured Design for Damask Rose" showing how the formulas are prepared by tracing over every line of the flower and leaves, and numbering them. *The Young Ladies' Journal Complete Guide to the Work-Table, 1885*

99 PAINTING ON GLASS. *c.* 1850. Version of Oriental or Pearl painting. The flower study was painted on glass in transparent oil stains, the background filled in with opaque light tints, and tin foil, after being crushed, was then smoothed out and placed behind flowers so that it glittered through the glass on the picture side. Framed in maple. *E. Tudor-Hart. Author's collection*

free-hand, but then was done with stencils, called 'theorems" or formulas, as all the work was theorematical. Flowers and fruit in baskets were the most popular subjects, stencilled in bright colours on white cotton velvet.

The earliest book on the craft was probably J. W. Alston's *Hints to Young Practitioners in the Study of Landscape Painting*, which was published in 1804. Instruction in the *Art of Painting on Velvet* was added to a new edition a year later.

The stencils were cut out of "horn" paper which was made by coating ordinary drawing paper with linseed oil, then brushing it with turpentine or varnish. The stencil was placed on the material and the open parts were covered with paint. The paint, of creamy consistency, was applied with a stiff brush in a downward circular motion. The detail work was done with India ink and a fine sable brush.

Painting on velvet caught on like wildfire in America. The *New York Commercial Advertiser* of 1821 advertised "E. B. Clayton No: 279 Broadway opposite Washington Hall has just received a few boxes of English Colors for painting on velvet warranted equal if not superior to any yet offered in this city."

A group of paper stencils selected from a large collection of stencils and brushes used in the vicinity of Tynnsboro, Massachusetts in the first half of the nineteenth century are in the Smithsonian Institution in New York, while some good examples of velvet paintings can be seen in the New York Historical Society's collection.

By 1830 *Godey's Lady's Book* was referring to painting on velvet and other materials as "Oriental Tinting" and "Poonah Work". Why? Perhaps because the work was said to have originated in the East, or my guess is that maybe "Poonah" came from poona, a snub-nosed brush used to paint through the hole in the stencil.

The Young Ladies' Journal Complete Guide to the Work-Table (1885) gives full instructions for painting on velvet, satin, silk, card, paper and wood, as well as a step-by-step guide to painting a damask rose, showing how the formulas were prepared:

For this, lay tracing-paper over the picture, and with a fine pencil trace *every line*, showing the shape of every leaf and stalk; then number every space which represents a leaf or stalk, taking care that leaves with the same number upon shall not be very close together.

Choose a small part of two leaves nearly opposite each other, and mark them off for "Conducting Points". When you have numbered every leaf, you will know how many Forms you will require for the group, and you must provide as many sheets of cartridge-paper, which you will number 1, 2, 3, etc.

Now take the cartridge-paper No. 1, and lay over it a piece of carbonized paper the same size, and over both lay the tracing; take an ivory stiletto, or other blunt-pointed instrument, and with it go over the outline of each leaf, etc., which is marked No. 1 on Diagram of Coloured Design. Repeat this process with each of the succeeding Forms.

The Conducting Points must be put in every Form, as they are the only guides for keeping each Form in its right place. See that you have a sufficient number of Forms, that the parts cut out may be at a convenient distance from each other, that in using the colours they may not run into each other, and also that the Forms may not be weakened by being cut too much in one part. Leaves and

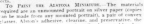

Making the Alstona Miniature. *Two glasses are used, and our first picture shows the work on the back glass, where the colours are applied in broad washes. The second shows the back of the glass on which the photograph of the subject is fixed. The work here consists of light washes of colours and touches on the high lights. The third picture shows the finished picture.*

The completed Glove Box with three miniatures inserted and Ribbon Work Decoration.

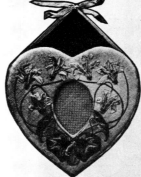

Cream Linen Photo Frame, worked with Pink Cyclamen.

Theatre Bag of White Silk, lined with Pink, and worked with Sweet Peas.

100 PAINTING ON GLASS. Early 1900s. The Alstona method used to make glass miniatures inserted on the top of a glove box also decorated with embroidery and ribbon work. *Needlecraft Monthly Magazine*

101 PAINTING ON RIBBON. Early 1900s. Cream linen photograph frame and a theatre bag decorated with painted ribbons. *Needlecraft Monthly Magazine*

flowers of various colours may be cut in the same Form, provided the different colours be far enough apart not to interfere with each other.

Each green leaf (except very small ones) must be cut in two Forms – that is, one side of it in one Form and one in another, by which means the space is divided so as to get a line for the middle vein. A small and very sharp pair of scissors must be used for cutting the apertures in the Forms. When diagrams have been traced and cut, they must be varnished twice over.

Instructions then follow as to how to make the varnish, how to mix the colours, and how to actually paint on the velvet using the forms.

To be of value in a collection, a velvet painting should be in good condition – dulling of colours will not detract from its value, but spots and tears do. They are rare (landscapes are rarer than fruit and flowers) but can be found. I saw a pair at a provincial antiques fair in Britain, and kicked myself when I got home for not buying them. At the time I did not know a great deal about them, and neither did the stall-holder.

Painting on glass comes into various categories. A transfer picture on glass is, briefly, the black print of a mezzotint engraving stuck on to the glass and coloured by hand after the removal of the paper pulp from the back of the print. After the colouring, the picture was varnished over, and the glass mounted and framed with the image on the reverse side.

Less ambitious were the glass pictures in which a design was painted by hand on the reverse side and then framed.

A third type of glass picture consists of a montage of coloured tinsel and silver paper which was pressed on to the glass and then framed. It is really this latter group which concerns us, as home-craft devotees.

There is a more detailed description of this type of simple glass painting by Frances Lichten in *Decorative Art of Victoria's Time*:

> Around 1850 the term "Oriental Painting" or "Pearl Painting" was transferred to a totally different technique – one in which flower studies were painted on glass in transparent oil stains, the background filled in with opaque light tints or with the solidity of lamp-black. Tin foil was crushed, then smoothed out and placed behind the floral forms previously indicated with line and thin coloured stain, so that it glittered attractively when viewed from the picture side.

I have a charming example in a maple frame which rather fits this admirable description. Obviously some of the pictures were not so good, and rather crudely done, Frances Lichten says that some of them are known now as American Primitives, which she considers "a far more attractive name than 'Victorian bungle' which describes them with more accuracy"!

The Alstona painting-on-glass method is described in the *Needlecraft Monthly Magazine* at the turn of the century: "To become successful in the art of Alstona painting one requires no other qualifications than a love for that which is artistic and beautiful, and a keen eye for colour."

Instructions were given for transforming an ordinary long, narrow chocolate box into a luxury container for gloves, covered in green silk with an embroidered top into which three miniatures in glass were inserted, and the whole thing trimmed with ribbons.

As Gertrude Jekyll, that lively landscape architect and gardener, who died in 1932 at the age of eighty-nine, would have said: "A free nothing into an artistic something." She it was who reckoned that "even for a lady, there was nothing at all demeaning in the attempt to convert an old barrel or tea chest into an elegant rustic support for flowers".

Painting on ribbon was another whimsy of the times. Said a *Needlecraft Monthly Magazine* of the early 1900s: "The ribbons obtainable at fancywork shops often fail to reproduce the exact shade of Nature, but here the paint-box fills in the gap, and gives to the dainty handiwork just that touch of individuality which the needle-lover delights to impart."

The ribbon was "modelled" into flowers, sewn into place, and then painted. Two examples shown in the magazine were a cream linen photograph frame adorned with a cyclamen made of pale pink ribbon, painted after working with a deeper pink shading to crimson at the base of each petal. The leaves and stalks are painted too, with the stalks a purplish crimson at the base, shading to pale green near the flowers;

the leaves are dark green with white markings. If oil paint was used, it was thinned very sparingly with paraffin; not too much, in case it ran into the background. For the flowers the paint was used quite thin, and was put on with light strokes down the petals.

Another example illustrated was a theatre bag, lined with pink and worked with sweet-peas. "In those pocketless days a little ribbon-worked bag should prove dear to the feminine heart."

Truly, most decorative items were dear to our Victorian woman – even patchwork, which started off as a simple craft, went on to heights of artistic glory. Read about it in the next chapter.

102 "Crazy" patchwork quilt initialled VR *c.* 1860. English. Made of pieces of colourful silks and velvets richly embroidered with floral and other motifs. Believed to have been embroidered by Queen Victoria at Osborne House. *Sotheby's Belgravia*

7

Something out of Nothing

PATCHWORK EXHIBITIONS
TEMPLATES AND SHAPES
PATCHWORK AMERICAN AND BRITISH STYLE
PATCHWORK MISCELLANY

"A thing of shreds and patches"

Mikado
W. S. GILBERT (1836–1911)

"It began to dawn upon me that I might be buried under an avalanche of quilts," wrote a bemused American woman in the early 1900s after she had suggested a patchwork quilt show at a small country fair.

"I wonder we could have been so benighted as to imagine we could do it in a day!" Her bright idea was so successful that it brought in "quilts by the dozen". After an hour she "sent in a general alarm to friends and kindred for help. . . By some magic of desperation we got those quilts on display, 118 of them, by one o'clock." So records Marie D. Webster in *Quilts, Their Story and How to Make Them.* I know just how her anonymous organizer felt!

I organized a Patchwork Competition and Exhibition for the National Federation of Women's Institutes at Sanderson House in London in 1970, and none of us would ever have believed that this fascinating, yet basically simple, country craft could come to life in such magnitude – over 800 items were sent in from all over Britain; 350 of them quilts, many quite old, with the rest of the patchwork made up of numerous small things ranging from bell pulls to bikinis.

Fortunately I had the resources of Sanderson, the famous fabric and wallpaper firm, to send out a "general alarm" to. But even so a fair amount of "magic of desperation" was needed to unwrap the patchwork, assemble it for the judges, then put it on display for the exhibition, and, most important of all, return all these precious, much-loved, irreplaceable items safely to their owners; and of course all this had to be fitted into the routine of an already too busy work-day!

One amusing incident was when many of the beautiful quilts were photographed stretched out flat on the ground outside the Sanderson factory, the photographer climbing on to a roof to get an aerial view. A party of visiting Spaniards (export customers) were touring the works at the time, and with numerous "bravos" and

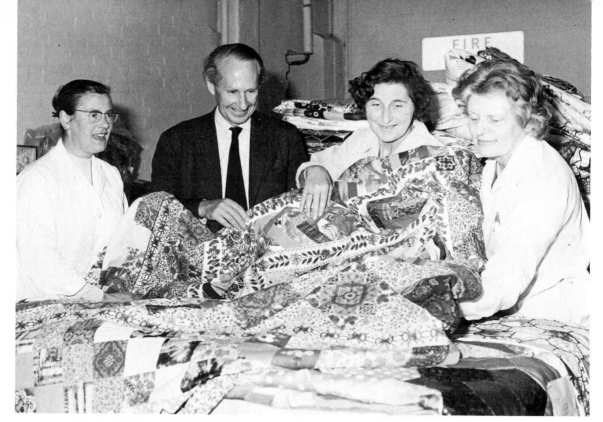

103 PATCHWORK EXHIBITION. National Federation of Women's Institutes judges (left to right) Mrs Betty Showler, Mrs Joan Field and Miss Dorothy Crampton examine over 800 entries for the Sanderson Patchwork Competition and Exhibition. Richard Bett, General Manager of Sanderson's Uxbridge factory looks on.

cries of admiration at the beautiful colours rushed for their cameras to record this quaint scene of British industry at work!

Fortunately the magic (and hard work of all concerned) worked, and the exhibition was acclaimed as "the biggest collection of patchwork in the world", "creating a whole new image for patchwork", and attracting an enormous number of visitors from all over Britain and overseas too.

The letters that came in with the entries made fascinating reading, revealing that long laborious painstaking effort had gone into making the patchwork.

Many of the quilts had taken years to complete. One, started in 1908 when the owner was eight years old, was made from ragbag pieces collected from her family and neighbours in the little village of Shirburn, Oxfordshire; it was lined with the pages of her old school books; she didn't finish it until she married, many years later.

One woman wrote that her quilt was made by her father's sister for her trousseau over a hundred years ago when she worked in a tie-maker's workroom in the City of London; so the patchwork was made completely of cuttings from ties! "It was never finished because her sweetheart died when she was making it."

One quilt was made by a sailor, James Cox, in 1865, while serving in H.M.S. *Victory*. "He made it for his sister, Mary Cox, who had brought him up, their mother having

104 PATCHWORK EXHIBITION. Mrs Ashcroft demonstrates how patchwork is made to Miss Festival of London Stores who visited the exhibition at Sanderson, Berners Street, London W.1.

105 PATCHWORK EXHIBITION. One of the patchwork quilts on display; note the charming border of flower baskets. *Richard Bett Collection*

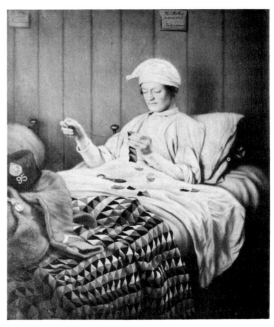

106 PATCHWORK. *c.* 1856. Painting by Thomas Wood of Private Walker in Fort Pitt Military Hospital, sewing a patchwork coverlet. *President and Council of the Royal College of Surgeons of England*

107 PATCHWORK QUILT. 1865–1866. Made by a sailor James Cox while serving 12 months in HMS Victory. It was made of pieces of red, black and white felt for his sister Mary and belongs to her grand-daughter Miss N. Jefferis of Bitton, Gloucestershire.

died when his sister was only 13", wrote the grand-daughter of Mary Cox. The quilt was an eye-catching piece made from red, black and white felt-cloth "diamonds", embroidered with flags.

Yes, men made patchwork too. Further proof of this is portrayed in a painting by Thomas Wood *c.* 1856, which shows a Private Walker in the Fort Pitt Military Hospital sitting up in bed and sewing a patchwork coverlet.

How did it all begin, this "thing of shreds and patches", this oddity which makes something out of nothing, turning waste into beauty, something which perhaps more than any other form of needlework possesses a warm, almost human quality?

It is thought that the Crusaders returning from Palestine in the eleventh century brought a kind of patchwork home to England in the form of gay banners. This was *applied* work though, where patches were sewn to the surface of the material, so that they formed a pattern either by their own shape and colour, or by the shape and colour of the ground materials.

According to the *Notes on Applied Work and Patchwork*, published by the Victoria and Albert Museum, the vogue for *mosaic* patchwork (fragments of material seamed edge to edge) cannot be traced for more than the last two centuries in England. "It would be gratifying to be able to follow its descent from the field of battle to the bedroom", says the writer.

and could the existence of a single English patchwork quilt of the sixteenth or seventeenth centuries be proved, then an English ancestry might be claimed for the whole American group.

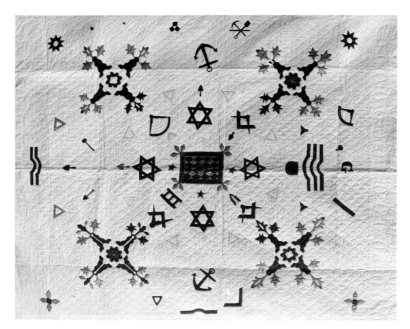

108 PATCHWORK QUILT. 1856. American. Appliqued quilt made by Mrs Rose Van Wart. Her husband cut the shapes for the various Masonic symbols out of different coloured cottons. *Newark Museum, Newark, New Jersey*

109 PATCHWORK QUILT. Nineteenth century. English. Hexagonal shaped patches in a double-sided quilt from Westmorland. Predominant colours are red and white. The reverse side is in a floral chintz of browns and greens. *Christopher Sykes Antiques*

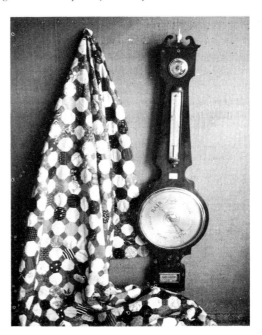

110 PATCHWORK QUILT. Nineteenth century. English. The octagonal patches are of blue, red, green and white, mixed in with plain red squares. *Christopher Sykes Antiques*

111 PATCHWORK PICTURE. Primitive patch picture by Elizabeth Allen. The Great Pyramid. *Crane Kalman Gallery*

But the fact remains that patchwork quilts do not seem to have been made in England until silks and printed cottons were common and cheap enough to be cut up before they were quite worn out. Thus from the end of the eighteenth century the fashion flourished, and all the poorer households had a quilt, patchwork on one side and plain, usually with the quilting stitches showing through on the other.

The writer goes on to affirm that it would be possible then to maintain that the later patchwork arose from the use of coloured materials for quilts, that it was a spontaneous peasant craft quite unrelated to upper-class fashions, except in so far as certain of its basic patterns are those of embroidery; and that it arose independently in England and the United States.

The word quilt, incidentally, is derived from the Latin *culcita*, which means a stuffed sack, mattress or cushion. Obviously the stuffing (wool, flock or down) between the two thicknesses of material, wool, silk or linen, gave extra warmth.

So when thrifty English women went to America in the eighteenth century they would surely make up the best parts of worn-out garments into pieces for bed covers, padded coverlets being needed for warmth in the New World as well as in England.

Before I go any further I will describe briefly the basic method of making patchwork, which still applies today:

1. A template is used as a pattern from which to cut a paper shape of each patch.
2. The patch is cut from a scrap of fabric sufficiently larger than the paper to give a practical turning, and then tacked to the paper.
3. The patches are sewn together, and the papers taken out.

In early patchwork the shapes were made without templates, i.e. those shapes from which the patches could be *accurately* cut into the shape required; materials were just cut and folded by hand. But quilting patterns needed templates to ensure the accurate repetition of an outline.

Many old templates were made by the men of the family, from a variety of materials, usually oak, tin and card, with others in silver, brass, copper, pewter and occasionally ivory and bone.

It is thought that when templates came in, the lining paper which was used for the patches came in too. The most popular shape, incidentally, are the hexagon, octagon, diamond and square which form the mosaic generally recognized as patchwork. There is no standard measurement for any shape, and it varies in proportion to the size of the work, a quilt obviously having a larger patch than a pincushion.

There are dozens of shapes and patterns, far too many to list here. You can read about them in the patchwork text books, study them in the museums, and gradually, if you start to collect, you will recognize them and begin to build up a representative collection.

It was the faded charm of a thick quilted spread (shown in the Sanderson exhibition) that first appealed to my collector's instinct.

I purchased this magnificent piece of work from the owner, a retired farmer. He had bought it in a sale at Eskdale, near his home in Holrook, Cumberland, many

112 PATCHWORK QUILT.
Nineteenth century. English. The centre panel of this quilt from Cumberland was printed to commemorate the Golden Jubilee of George III in 1810. The corners of the quilt have medallions celebrating the Golden Jubilee of Queen Victoria in 1887. *Author's collection*

113 COMMEMORATIVE PANELS FOR PATCHWORK. English. Close-up of the centre panel of the Cumberland quilt, specially printed to celebrate the Golden Jubilee of George III in 1810. on the left is a close-up of medallions printed to celebrate Queen Victoria's Golden Jubilee in 1887. These were added later to the corners of the quilt.

years ago – as one of four for less than a pound (a little over a dollar). There can have been no doubt of their warmth-exuding qualities; three had been used as cow rugs, with only this one retained for a bed cover!

The exact date of the quilt was not known. But the unusual centre panel was printed from a polychrome wood block designed to commemorate the golden jubilee of George III in 1810. Cotton manufacturers printed these decorative panels from 1800 until about 1816. They were designed specially as ready-made centre panels to be sewn in the centre of a coverlet. (To find out more about them, read *Patchwork* by

Averil Colby, one of the foremost authorities on the technique, design and history of patchwork.)

The panel is oval shaped, and contains a basket overflowing with a profusion of lilies, roses, marigolds and convolvulus, on a red ground. The basket is borded with acorns and oak leaves. Set in the border at the bottom is the wording "G–50–R". The Rose of England and the Thistle of Scotland flank the side of the date, and above is a bunch of shamrock.

The quilt was probably made in stages, because on the corners are tiny medallions commemorating the golden jubilee of Queen Victoria in 1887, featuring the crowned head of the monarch. Presidential slogans printed on textiles were the American equivalent, which often found their way into patchwork.

My next buy was some examples of "crazy" patchwork. This type of work took its name from the haphazard arrangement of the various pieces of brightly coloured fabrics put together in crazy paving fashion, giving a kaleidoscope effect. Feather-stitching was used to cover the raw edges of the patches.

The things I have are probably mid-Victorian: a coffee-pot cover, a tea-cosy and matching egg-cosies. Made of rich, brightly coloured pieces of velvet, which have been feather- or blanket-stitched together, the items are edged with braid. Just to make sure you know which cover is for the teapot (apart from the shape), there is a clock face and the letter "T" embroidered on the front.

A beautiful example of applied patchwork (that is, pieces in the design are cut out and *applied* to a plain ground) that I have is a double spread in rich silks with velvet. Very fragile, the sides have been taken in to prevent the silk from splitting further. There is a silk fringe at the top and bottom.

On a broad border adjacent to the fringing are stars with eight points, their centres filled in with patches of velvet. These stars, and the richness of the colours (hardly dimmed by the years), give the spread an exotic Eastern effect.

It was actually made by a woman born in London in 1865 who went to finishing school in France. Her father was Henry Bishop, who was the owner of Gunters, the famous tea shop in Mayfair, alas now no more. With the coverlet the owner sent me a letter written by the woman to her father when she was a young girl, which makes delightful reading.

To get to know more about patchwork, you should visit the museums that include it in their display of needlework. The Victoria and Albert has a fine collection of patchwork, so does the Welsh Folk Museum near Cardiff and the American Museum in Britain at Claverton Manor, Bath.

The American Museum has a splendid coverlet made by a Quaker, Dr Sarah Rogers, one of the earliest women physicians in Philadelphia, Pennsylvania. It was awarded a silver label inscribed "Premium to S.T.M. for Silk Quilt 10th No 1852", at the State Fair, Trenton, New Jersey.

The coverlet is called "Tumbling Blocks", and the fascinating, quite three-dimensional design is a giant star of silk "boxes" formed of two diamond-shaped striped, figured, brocaded and plain silk pieces combined with the black diamonds on a grey and pink striped ground.

In the Smithsonian Institute there is an elaborately designed quilt made by a Mrs Mary Green Moran in Baltimore, Maryland, when she was a bride of eighteen. It features a flower-basket pattern with the foundation material of white silk, and the work is done with coloured silks and raised or padded applied work.

The quilt is composed of thirteen square blocks containing the basket motifs and twelve triangular pieces of embroidered flower patterns. The blocks are joined to three-inch bands of embroidered silk with a strawberry-vine design, while the outer border of the quilt consists of a seven-inch band decorated with a running-vine pattern.

Dating quilts is not easy. Sometimes you find the original paper patterns still in the back of the patchwork. They could be newspapers with advertisements that give a clue to the date, and place where it was made, old bills, letters and so on.

116 APPLIED PATCHWORK.
Nineteenth century. English.
Silk spread with patches of silk
and velvet. Silk fringe top and
bottom. *Author's collection*

Highwood Hill
My dear Papa
  This afternoon
I am going with
Aunt Ada to London
to stay with her
for a few days.
I want to see
you very much in-

deed, we all wish
you many many
happy returns
of the 15ᵗʰ. We
all had cham-
pagne to drink
Uncle Edgars good
health. Please

give my best love
to Aunt Maria. We
are all quite well,
and with many
kisses from your
loving little
daughter
      Helen

117 LETTER. By the worker of the applied patchwork coverlet. Helen's father was Henry
Bishop the owner of Gunter's the famous Mayfair tea shop.

American "friendship" quilts were signed and often dated on each block by the makers. Mainly around the 1850s, these bedcovers, also known as "presentation" or "album" quilts, were made and given to a member of a community by friends to mark a special occasion.

In the Newark Museum, New Jersey, which has a marvellous collection of quilts and counterpanes dating from 1680 to the turn of the twentieth century, is an

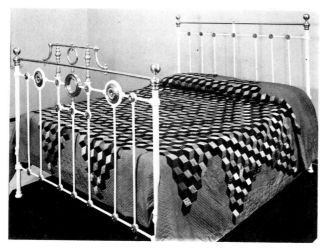

118 PATCHWORK COVERLET. 1852. American. Made by a Quaker, Dr Sarah Rogers one of the earliest women physicians in Philadelphia, Pennsylvania. It was awarded a silver label at the State Fair, Trenton, New Jersey. The coverlet is called "Tumbling Blocks". *American Museum in Britain*

119 PATCHWORK QUILT. Nineteenth century. American. Made by Mrs Mary Green of Baltimore Maryland when she was a bride of 18. It features an elaborate version of a flower basket pattern in coloured silks. *Smithsonian Institution, Washington DC*

enchanting model of a Quaker quilting party, made about 1870 by Martha S. Stedman of Elizabeth, New Jersey.

The heads of the figures are hickory nuts. On the quilt top is a red pincushion. As a young girl Martha Stedman, the donor's mother, had acquaintances among the Quakers and frequently attended Quaker Meetings.

The quilting frame in this model is not the usual type and would be less convenient than frames that rested on chair backs. However, this frame was made by a relative of Martha Stedman's, presumably according to her specifications and copying those Martha had seen at Quaker parties. Quilters frequently stood to do their quilting, especially when starting from the centre. The lower bar on each side, stretching between the ends of the framework, could be used to stand on as a convenience in reaching. When the quilter stood it was not necessary to roll the frames over so frequently, an advantage since rolling tended to ripple the layers of cloth.

Only four to six women could work together comfortably at a quilting frame; often a housewife waited until she had two or more tops ready for the frames, then she would have a party and invite the neighbourhood women. The men joined the group for supper and an evening of games, which accounts for the presence of the Elder in the group.

There was communal quilt-making in the cottages and farmhouses of Britain too. A daughter in a family had to help quilt the coverlets to use on the beds in her home when she was married. She had to start at an early age, for the target was a baker's dozen – thirteen – for the wedding chest; the last one was the bride's quilt. An old Devon rhyme goes:

> "At your quilting maids, don't dally,
> Quilt quickly if you would marry,
> A maid who is quiltless at twenty-one
> Never shall greet her bridal sun!"

87

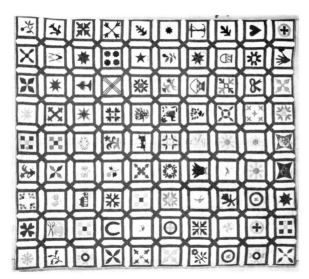

120 PATCHWORK QUILT. 1876. American. Friendship quilt worked by the Demarest family. *Newark Museum, New Jersey*

121 QUAKER QUILTING PARTY. 1870. American. Group of figures and quilt on frame made by Martha S. Stedman, Elizabeth, New Jersey. *Newark Museum, New Jersey*

122 QUILTING BEE. Nineteenth century. American. From a drawing by H. W. Pierce. *Old-Time New England Bulletin*

Marriage quilts were made in America as well, and "quilting bees" were held, parties at which friends of the engaged girl gathered to put the finishing touches.

In the informative catalogue issued by the Newark Museum an appropriate comment on one of the American Star of Bethlehem designs (a central eight-pointed star of diamond-shaped pieces) is:

123 PATCHWORK QUILT. Nineteenth century. American. Star of Bethlehem pattern—eight pointed star in printed cottons. *Victoria and Albert Museum*

124 PATCHWORK. Pieces of unfinished Victorian patchwork. *Author's collection*

125 PATCHWORK DRESSING GOWN; Nineteenth century. English. Woman's robe made entirely of small patches. *National Federation Women's Institute collection*

126 PATCHWORK DRESSING GOWN. Nineteenth century. English. Man's robe made entirely of large hexagon patches of chiné and plain silks. *Victoria and Albert Museum*

127 PATCHWORK SMOKING JACKET. Late Victorian jacket in crazy patchwork with taffeta patches oversewn in feather stitch. *Derek & Ursula Powell Antiques*

128 PATCHWORK MISCELLANY. Contemporary. Selection patchwork articles—pin cushions, tea-cosy and needle case. *National Federation Women's Institutes collection*

129 PATCHWORK QUILT. Contemporary. English. Worked by Mrs Joan Bergh, Shepton Mallet; made of 7,000 ⅝ths of an inch hexagons on a white waffle weave cotton background. Predominant colourings orange, red and yellow with white and black. *Winner National Federation of Women's Insitutes Patchwork Competition*

90

While it might seem difficult, today, to figure out how to cut a square into eight perfectly matched diamonds, it seems to have been no problem for our great-grandmothers.

Perhaps the answer lies in the art of the cut-paper picture. . . . In Revolutionary days the cutting of stiff paper to form ornamental designs was considered a high accomplishment. The art was known as Papyrotamia and one skilled in cutting was a papyrotamist.

Of course, remember those skilful paper patterns of the first chapter?

What should you pay for patchwork? The main thing to consider is that no realistic price can be put upon a hand-made object which may have taken months, usually years, to make. Patchwork probably owes its existence to the fact that it has never had any real commercial value. The time required to make a true patchwork quilt which would show a reasonable profit to the worker has kept this traditional work comparatively safe from the money-making business.

In antique markets and country shops I have bought small pieces of unfinished Victorian patchwork which will make up into cushion covers as well as quilts; and you can look for late Victorian smoking jackets and dressing gowns in patchwork as well as numerous small items such as pincushions and needlecases.

Remember that today's patchworks are the antiques of tomorrow. The superb quilt made by Mrs Joan Bergh of Shepton Mallet, Somerset, with a diamond design using over seven thousand $\frac{5}{8}$ths of an inch hexagonal templates, which took her over seven months to make (a remarkably short time really!), and won her first prize in the Women's Institutes Competition, is obviously already an heirloom of the future.

8

Charlotte, Una and Other Women

NEEDLEWORK PICTURES IN WOOL, SILK AND HAIR
FISHING LADIES – BOSTON-STYLE
MOURNING AT THE TOMB
BIBLICAL BYWAYS
COLLECTOR'S ALBUM – EVERY PICTURE TELLS A STORY

"She excelled in needlework, she painted in water colour – of such is the kingdom of heaven"

Inscription on tomb of eighteenth-century woman

Because work is old, it is not necessarily beautiful. So observed M. S. Lockwood and E. Glaister in *Art Embroidery* in 1878.

But as they went on to admit, there is a certain nostalgia about old needlework:

the colours soften and mellow; the linen takes a creamy tint, the stitches fit into their places in the long companionship of years; and the mystery of past generations – of the busy fingers quiet now, of hopes failed or fulfilled, of stories that must ever be untold – hangs about the fragments that we tenderly handle and preserve.

I think that just about sums up the charm of old needlework, whether it is good or bad. Collectors of pictorial embroidery, particularly those operating within a modest price range, will find it easy to derive pleasure from the naïveté and simplicity that is often part of the charm of old needlework. Perfection cannot be all when the hand that wielded the needle was not always as skilled as one might wish it to be.

The quality of the work in the **needlework pictures** that I am featuring in this chapter varies enormously. But they do present an overall view of what could be "shaped and wrought" with the needle.

An enchanting scene of rustic merriment, believed to be either North Italian or Austrian *c.* 1710, was on Mayorcas' Stand at a Grosvenor House Antiques Fair. What a beautiful picture in needlework it is! Take a magnifying glass to the photograph and note the delightful little details – the man puffing contentedly away at his pipe, the woman sitting on the steps with her bunch of household keys dangling at her waist, the men quaffing their drink, the dog with his bone watched by a fierce-looking cat.

130 PICTORIAL EMBROIDERY. *c.* 1710. North Italian or Austrian "laid" stitch on canvas
in the manner of David Teniers, depicting scenes of rustic merriment. *Mayorcas*

131 WOOL PICTURE. Eighteenth century. English. Portrait of Napoleon worked on canvas with coloured wools in long and short stitches by Mary Linwood (1775–1845). *Victoria and Albert Museum*

132 WOOL PICTURE.
Early 1800s. English. By
Mary Dale of
Hemmingford.

It is pictorial embroidery at its best, in the subdued mellow colourings of the countryside, with even the details of the sky and the faces stitched in.

Equally fine, in its way, is the portrait of Napoleon Bonaparte (to be seen in the Victoria and Albert) worked on canvas with coloured wools in long and short stitches, by Miss Mary Linwood of Leicester (1755–1845). This work was but one of many, mostly full-sized copies of celebrated paintings that were first sketched by Miss Linwood on a ground of thick tammy cloth (a strong woollen fabric) woven specially for her, and worked in soft crewels in shades dyed to her order. Her study of Napoleon was actually made from a sketch she made when she visited Paris. The irregular straight stitches used were meant to imitate the strokes of an artist's brush.

Miss Linwood was also an author, composer, director of a girl's boarding school, and had been received by the Empress of Russia.

The first of her exhibitions was held in 1787, and *The Times* declared the whole effect "almost magical". Her "Gallery of Pictures in Worsted" was opened in 1798 and for nearly fifty years was one of the sights of London. Her copies of famous paintings after Sir Joshua Reynolds, Stubbs and Gainsborough (around sixty in all) were said to be more admired by the public than the paintings themselves.

133 WOOL PICTURE. Nineteenth century. English. Probably worked by a sailor. *Victoria and Albert Museum travelling exhibition 'Victorian Popular Art'*

134 PICTORIAL EMBROIDERY. THE FISHING LADY. Eighteenth century. American. A "chimney-piece" worked by Eunice Bourne of New England. *Museum of Fine Arts Boston*

But after her death the sale of her "paintings" realized only about a thousand pounds although she had once refused three thousand guineas for her copy of Carlo Dolci's *Salvator Mundi*; this she bequeathed to Queen Victoria and it is still in the Royal Collection. Her work was out of fashion; and by the turn of the twentieth century Mrs Emily Leigh Lowes, in her *Chats on Old Lace and Embroidery*, had some very harsh things to say about her: "Would that she had never been born!... Death was too good for Miss Linwood. The usual boiling oil would have been a fitter end!"

Miss Linwood was not the only one to work masterpieces in wool. There was also Miss Mary Knowles (1733–1807), a Quaker who won the esteem of George III and Queen Charlotte, and promptly worked an elaborate study of the king from a painting of him by John Zoffany (1773–1810). This is displayed next to the Linwood Napoleon in the Victoria and Albert, and suffers slightly by comparison, because although the same irregular long and short stitches are used, they are rather larger and the effect is not quite so much of needle-painting.

For the collector there are wool pictures of English rural scenes to be found – I have seen two done by a Mary Dale of Hemmingford, probably around the 1800s.

135 NEEDLEWORK PICTURE. Dated 1817. American. Washington memorial scene with Mount Vernon in the background. Worked in silk and chenille. Gilt box frame, with painted black border inscribed in gilt along the bottom. "In Memory of Washington Elizabeth Lane Fecit 1817". *The Henry Francis du Pont Winterthur Museum*

Some woolwork pictures which were done by sailors can occasionally be found. The best were remarkable for their intricacy of detail and boldness of design, with ships obviously the most popular subjects. Sometimes the ships are very attractively worked, with the three-deckers still proudly in full sail, while showing the funnels and smoke that reveal the conversion to steam.

I saw a fine wool picture by a Gunner G. Baldie of the Royal Artillery at the Crane Kalman Gallery in London's Knightsbridge. Crudely done perhaps, it had a naïve, natural quality, and was indeed included in an exhibition of English Naïve Paintings. As Andras Calman said in the catalogue of this show held at Simpson's

136 NEEDLEWORK PICTURE. Eighteent[h]
century. English. Typical mourning at th[e]
tomb scene. Note the girl's large white hand
kerchief held at the side of her dress. *Filkin*
Author's collection

in Piccadilly: "Discovering these pictures can be likened to the pleasures of fishing. From time to time one comes up with an exciting and rewarding catch."

At which point it is appropriate to mention the American needlework pictures known as *The Fishing Lady and Boston Common* group of related embroideries.

These are embroideries representing the finest type of American needlework, with a fascinating relationship in design. At least sixty-five examples have been recorded and photographed, and the photographs are in the Textile Department of the Boston Museum of Fine Arts.

The museum owns a fine pictorial "chimney-piece" featuring the actual "fishing lady" herself (some feature shepherdesses), worked by a Eunice Bourne. The pictures are believed to have been the work of young women in their late teens, daughters of prosperous New England families who probably attended Boston finishing schools where fine needlework was a necessary accomplishment. The history of the pictures has been effectively summed up in an article by Nancy Graves Cabot in *The Antique Book*, and makes fascinating reading. In it she reminds us that "to enjoy pictorial embroidery it is best at the outset to forget the conventions of perspective, else one will lose the piquancy of surprise at flowers, butterflies and houses of equal size, and the charm of much irrelevant detail".

Collectors could well make their own group of related subjects in needlework pictures. There are plenty of the part embroidered (wool, silk and hair), part colour-washed pictures of the late eighteenth and early nineteenth century around.

98

137 NEEDLEWORK PICTURE. Eighteenth century. English. Charlotte mourning at the
tomb of Werther. *E. Tudor-Hart. Author's collection*

138 NEEDLEWORK PICTURE. Eighteenth century. English. After a painting by Angelica Kaufmann. Fame Adorning Shakespeare's Tomb. *Victoria and Albert Museum*

139 NEEDLEWORK PICTURE. Eighteenth century. English. Another version of Fame Adorning Shakespeare's Tomb. *Private collection*

140 NEEDLEWORK PICTURE. 1774. American. Queen of Sheba Admiring the Wisdom of Solomon. *Smithsonian Institute, Washington DC*

141 NEEDLEWORK PICTURE. 1750–75. American. Biblical scene, possibly the meeting of David and Absolom. Worked by Anne Carlisle, Leesbury, New Jersey in silk thread. Note the detail—reclining camel at right; man fishing at left, shepherds playing flutes and tending flocks in the corners, and in the background, tents, trees, towers, birds and clouds. *The Henry Francis du Pont Winterthur Museum*

142 NEEDLEWORK PICTURE. 1800–1820. American. "And the Daughter of Pharoah came down to wash herself at the river; and when she saw the Ark among the flags she sent her maid to fetch it. Exod. Ch. 2 Verse 5." Predominant colours of beige, light brown, green and blue, worked in silk. Framed in gilt with white border on which is inscribed "Wrought by Mary S. Crafts at Mrs Saunders & Miss Bead's Academy Dorchester". The back board has a label with the words "Mary Sibyl Crafts/Born in Princeton, Mass/Jan 5, 1788". *The Henry Francis du Pont Winterthur Museum*

Based on paintings and engravings of the period, they were originally bought ready-drawn on pale taffeta grounds with such details as face, hands and clouded skies painted in with water colours. Only the landscape and figures were embroidered with coloured silks or wools, mainly in long and short satin and stem stitches. Sometimes the faces, hands and arms were carefully cut out of paper and pasted on the silk or satin ground.

Sentimental subjects abounded, with various **mourning at the tomb** tableaux. A popular American one of the early 1800s was a Washington memorial scene with women weeping at a large white urn on a square pedestal.

A subject that proved astonishingly popular, and which is found in varying degrees of stitchery, some fine and some indifferent, is that of Charlotte mourning at the tomb of Werther. He was the sentimental hero of Goethe's romantic novel *The Sorrows of Werther* who was so overcome by his unrequited love for Lotte that he took his life.

Another popular scene of a classically draped female strewing flowers on a tomb is *Fame Adorning Shakespeare's Tomb*, after a painting by the Swiss artist Angelica Kaufmann (1741–1807). There is one example in the Victoria and Albert, on taffeta with silk embroidery, with painted face, arms and feet, believed to be early nineteenth-century. An

101

143 NEEDLEWORK PICTURE.
Early nineteenth century.
American. The Baptism of
Ethiopian Enuch by St Thomas.
*Smithsonian Institute, Washington
DC*

144 NEEDLEWORK PICTURE.
Nineteenth century. English.
Jesus with the Woman at the
Well. *Chloe Antiques. Author's
collection*

interesting contrast is one I have seen in a private collection, where the shading of the garments is not quite so subtle. The action is the same, but the expression on the painted face a little different.

Therle Hughes, in *English Domestic Needlework 1660–1860*, points out: "There has always been a tendency in considering old embroideries to stress the changes in taste and technique, but it is important to recognise the extent and duration of transitional work."

145 NEEDLEWORK PICTURE. Nineteenth century. English. Believed to have been embroidered by Lady Hamilton, it is meant to represent Emma on the arm of Lord Nelson at Merton Park, Surrey where her husband, Lord Hamilton, completed the menage à trois. *National Maritime Museum, Greenwich*

146 NEEDLEWORK PICTURE. First quarter nineteenth century. English. Shepherdess with her flock resting by a tree and reading. *City of Sheffield Museum*

147 NEEDLEWORK PICTURE. Black stitches on cream silk give a stippled effect. Probably St Francis of Assissi. *The Antique Supermarket. Author's collection*

This particularly applies to **biblical themes**, which could also form the basis of an interesting pictorial embroidery collection. Many of the mid eighteenth century religious figures were a left-over from contemporary Stuart rather than ancient or Eastern. Solomon greeting the Queen of Sheba is every inch a Stuart king, and David and Absolam have the same stocky Stuart flavour. Also, how long were embroideries kept at home, unfinished, and handed down from one member of the family to another?

A needlework picture of the daughter of Pharaoh going down to wash, 1800–12, has the woman dressed in what could be a high-waisted flowing gown of the Regency period, but reasonably sacred garb is sported by St Thomas baptizing an Ethiopian eunuch (Virginia, early nineteenth century); and Jesus with the woman at the well looks suitably attired. This picture brings to life the words in the Gospel of St John, chapter four: "Now Jacob's well was there. Jesus therefore, being wearied with his journey, sat thus on the well. . . . There cometh a woman of Samaria to draw water: Jesus saith unto her, Give me to drink."

For the lover of Nelson relics, the needlework picture believed to have been worked by the fair hand of Lady Hamilton is in the National Maritime Museum in Greenwich. It shows Emma on the arm of Nelson at Merton Park in Surrey, where her husband, Sir William Hamilton, completed the *ménage à trois*.

With Emma is a pet dog. Animals nearly always had their place in the pastoral needlework scene. Dogs, cats, sheep and lions (more of the latter later).

An oval picture of a shepherdess in the City of Sheffield Museum has the usual painted face and sky, with the trees painted in too, but they are also embroidered with tiny running stitches which are closer together where the effect of shadow was needed.

The foundation material is silk which is embroidered in silk thread using satin stitch with the exceptions of the tree trunk and the sheep. The tree trunk is formed of what appears to be silk chenille couched down; it is quite thick and stands out strongly from the background. The sheep appear to be formed of unspun wool, perhaps gathered from bushes in the countryside; again, this wool is couched down at intervals. (Couching consists of a strand of cord, or of several strands of silk or wool, laid together and caught down by stitches of the same or some other material at equal distance.)

Before I go back to the lion, let me refer to another type of eighteenth- and nineteenth-century embroidery, known as **print** work, in which detailed copies of line and stipple engravings were worked on white or cream taffeta.

In the most ambitious of these, almost every line of the engraving was reproduced in silks shaded from black to pale grey and cream. In others the more subtle effects were achieved with the help of sepia colour.

An oval picture I have, of what could be St Francis of Assissi, looks like a print, but is all worked in tiny stitches in black thread on cream silk.

Another oval picture I have shows the line and stipple effect even more strikingly; it is of a lady with a lion, which could be based on Spenser's Una from his *Faery Queen*.

Spenser says that while Una was seeking St George she sat to rest herself, when a lion rushed suddenly out of a thicket, with gaping mouth and lashing tail; but as he drew near he was awestruck and, laying aside his fury, kissed her feet and licked her hands; for "beauty can master strength, and truth subdue vengeance". (The lion of course, being the emblem of England which waits upon Truth.)

The lion followed Una as a dog, but is regrettably slain later by Sansloy, who carries Una off into the woods. Una is rescued by fauns and satyrs who attempt to worship her but, being restrained, pay adoration to her donkey. If you look at the right of the picture there is the animal's head.

I have also seen Una in a full-colour embroidery picture – she has her lion with her, but no donkey.

The background to needlework pictures is varied and interesting, and there are still plenty of them to be searched out from shop and market.

Here is a *Collector's Album* of needlework pictures in wool, silk and sometimes hair, all from private collections or shops, not museums, all of which have a story to tell:

149 NEEDLEWORK PICTURE. Dated on back 1788. English. Small Oval. Country scene, with woman in cart, and man drawing horse, outside the thatched farm house. All in russet autumnal colourings of green, brown and orange. *Charles Toller. Author's collection*

150 NEEDLEWORK PICTURE. *c.* 1790. Country scene of mother and child. The boy is feeding the pigs. The pet bird is in its cage, safely out of reach of the watchful cat below. *Gloria Antica*

JEMMY'S RETURN.

151 NEEDLEWORK PICTURE. *c.* 1790 English. *Jemmy's Return.* Copy of picture attributed to Robert Sayer 1786, and reproduced in Robinson's *The British Tar in Fact and Fiction*. One of a pair, the other is *Jemmy's Farewell*. The story is supposed to be that immortalised in the ballad of *Auld Robin Gray*, verses by Lady Lindsay in the *Golden Treasury*. Jamie went to sea to make his fortune, but was shipwrecked and reported drowned, so Jennie his sweetheart reluctantly married Auld Robin Gray who promised to support her impoverished parents. Then Jamie returned unexpectedly— hence Jennie's distress and her lament:

> "I daurna think on Jamie, for that would be a
> sin;
> But I'll do my best a gude wife to be,
> For Auld Robin Gray he is kind unto me."

This fascinating information came from a Miss Payne of Thornton Heath, Surrey, who wrote in to *Country Life* after the owner of the picture, Commander Patrick Tailyour of Great Easton, Leicestershire, had asked in the correspondence columns of the magazine for more details. Further information came from G. P. Rye, the curator of the public library and museum at Weston-super-Mare, Somerset.

"About 1770 William Leeves, then an ensign in the 1st Regiment of Foot Guards, composed an air for the ballad which subsequently gained considerable popularity. It was officially published by William Leeves, when in Holy Orders, in 1812 together with a Collection on Sacred Airs. The Rev. Leeves, who was Rector of Wrington (Somerset) from 1779 to 1828, built a cottage on the strand at Weston-super-Mare, in the 1790s, and a portion of it still stands with its thatched roof on the sea front.

Mr A. W. Moon, grand-daughter of Rev. Leeves and wife of Dr W. Moon, inventor of the Moon system of reading for the blind, published in 1873 a history of this ballad and its air in *In Memoriam.*"

152 NEEDLEWORK PICTURE OVAL. *c.* 1800.
English. Pastoral scene of woman with two children,
gathering flowers. *Gloria Antica*

153 PAIR OF NEEDLEWORK PICTURES. *c.* 1800. English.
One is another version of Werther's Lotte strewing flowers on
his tomb. Note the interesting patchwork effect on the ground.
The other has the woman with the sheep, and mountains in
the background, which makes me wonder whether it is English. She has a counterpart in the New York Historical Society
collection. The lady with the sheep was a popular subject
though; there is another version, almost identical, without the
mountains, in Mrs Lowes' *Chats on Old Lace & Needlework*, 1908
Mrs Lowes also refers to the method of working the dress,
which is similar to that in a "dressed print".

"Another pretty style which we seldom meet with was some
part of the picture covered with the almost obsolete 'aerophane', a kind of chiffon or crape. A certain part of the draperies was worked on the silk ground, without any attempt
at finish. This was covered with aerophane, and outlined so
as to attach it to the figure. This again was worked on to very
happy effects, very fine darning stitches making the requisite
depths of shading."

154 NEEDLEWORK PICTURE. *c.* 1800. English. Girl carrying basket, fishing rod and her "catch". Embroidered in fine
long and short stitch in silk on satin background. *The Embroiderers' Guild*

108

156 NEEDLEWORK PICTURE. Early 1800s. English. Girl with drum in a country scene. *Charles Toller. Author's collection*

155 NEEDLEWORK PICTURE. Early 1800s. English. Girl at spinning wheel outside cottage with cat. *Filkins. Author's collection*

157 NEEDLEWORK PICTURE. Early nineteenth century. English. *The Castle in Danger*. Three golden haired children building a house of cards, interrupted by an adult. *Grosvenor Antiques*

158 PAIR NEEDLEWORK PICTURES. *c.* 1815. *Mother's Pride* and *Father's Joy*. The boy is the one with the high-waisted Regency dress! They are presumably copied from engravings published 1815 by T. Palser, Westminster Bridge. *The Dower House*

159 WOOLWORK PICTURE. *c.* 1815. English. Girl with pitcher. All worked in muted hues of browns and pinks. *Charles Toller. Author's collection*

160 NEEDLEWORK PICTURE. Dated 1840 on back. French. All worked in brightly coloured chenilles. Two couples at Vincennes. *Delaney. Author's collection*

161 NEEDLEWORK PICTURE. 1796. English. Worked by Eliza Skinner. Circular and mounted in original frame. Embroidered in straight stitches in hair and silk. Portrait of a man wearing a turban. *The Embroiderers' Guild Collection*

162 PEN AND INK DRAWING. Note the similarity of the previous needlework picture with this drawing by John Hamilton ARA 1741–1779 called *The Aga of the Janisseries* inscribed Charlotte Augusta Matilda who commissioned it. *Fry Gallery* (featured *The Price Guide to English Watercolours 1750–1900. The Antique Collectors' Club*)

163 NEEDLEWORK PICTURE. Eighteenth century. Embroidery on silk typical of the chinoiserie flavour of the period. *E. Tudor-Hart*

164 NEEDLEWORK PICTURE. English. Scene from Shakespeare's Othello worked by a pupil of Mrs Crouche's school in Andover 1810 (written on back). *W. W. Warner (Antiques). Author's collection*

165 NEEDLEWORK PICTURE. Eighteenth century. English. I have seen several versions of this woman with her dog. Very soulful, she sits with her head in her hand, with large rocks behind her. Is she another Una? *Antique Supermarket. Contemporary frame by John Campbell, Chelsea, Author's collection*

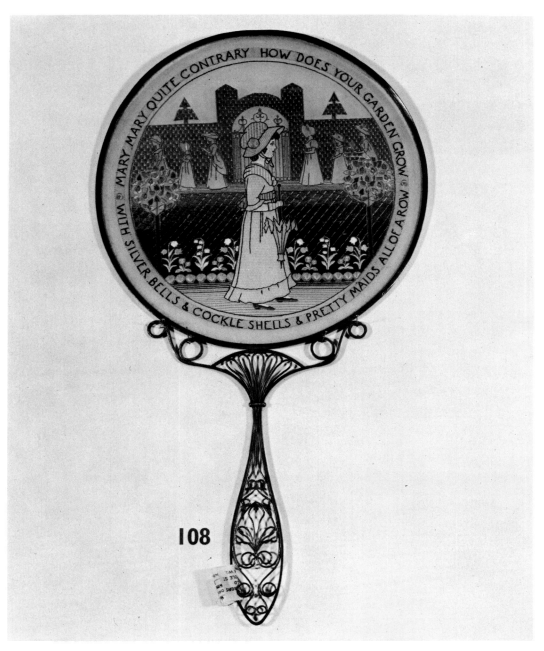

MARY MARY QUITE CONTRARY HOW DOES YOUR GARDEN GROW
WITH SILVER BELLS & COCKLE SHELLS & PRETTY MAIDS ALL OF A ROW

108

166 HANDSCREEN. 1910. English. On fine white gauze Mary, Mary Quite Contrary is worked in filo floss of greens, blues, white and sand, with salmon coloured roses. The stitchery including "laid" work, stem stitch, darning patterns and satin stitch is worked so that the design is reversible. The lettering is worked in black back stitch. Worked for the City and Guilds of London Institute examination by Kathleen Powell. *One Thousand Years of Embroidery Exhibition, Celanese House 1971. The Embroiderers' Guild*

9

Wool, Bead, Hair and Fish

BERLIN WOOL WORK
BEADWORK
MOOSE HAIR WORK
FISHSCALE EMBROIDERY

"She died at a good old age, having wrought out the Bible in tapestry."

UNKNOWN

When we think of the many years which English women have spent over those wickedly hideous Berlin-wool pictures, working their bad drawing and vilely crude colours in those awful canvases, and imagining that they were earning undying fame as notable women for all the succeeding ages . . .

So wrote Emily Leigh Lowes in 1908.

Continuing her castigation she went on to refer to "pleasing little horrors" considered suitable for the drawing-room, mainly of religious subjects, and finished with: "Needlework as a national art is as dead as the proverbial door-nail."

Mrs Lowes was not alone in her condemnation, yet **Berlin wool work** does have a charm of its own, and time has muted the once garish Berlin wool colours.

Why Berlin? From the city of its origin. Around 1810, a German woman got her husband to print her some designs on paper for embroidery, which were so popular they became a commercial venture and were imported into Britain and America.

The designs were drawn out on squared paper and hand-coloured, with every square representing a stitch. They were then copied square by square and stitch by stitch on to square-meshed canvas, by counting.

Cross or tent stitches were worked in worsted wools called "zephyr" yarns in Germany, but called Berlin wools in England.

The craze for the work reached its height around 1840 when over fourteen thousand different patterns had been imported into England. Although it was on the decline by the end of the century, even in 1885 *The Young Ladies' Journal Complete Guide to the Work-Table* gave full details of a variety of stitches that could be used.

Religious pictures, particularly subjects from the Old Testament, can be found by collectors. To get your eye in you could take a look at some of those in museum collections.

"The Last Supper", after Leonardo da Vinci, is a dramatic example which can

113

168 BERLIN WOOL WORK. English. *The Last Supper* after Leonardo da Vinci, all worked in Berlin wools. Signed and dated Mrs J. Morris, 1851. *Bethnal Green Museum*

167 BERLIN WOOL WORK. The designs were drawn on squared paper with every square representing a stitch. They were then copied square by square and stitch by stitch on to square meshed canvas, by counting. *The Young Ladies Journal Complete Guide to the Work-Table, 1885*

170 BERLIN WOOL WORK; Nineteenth century. English. Abraham offering Isaac, worked in Berlin wools. *City Museum, Stoke-on-Trent*

169 BERLIN WOOL WORK. *c.* 1850. English. The Anointing of David worked in Berlin wools. *Bowes Museum*

114

171 BERLIN WOOL WORK. Mid-nineteenth century. English. Joseph sold by his Brethren. Wrought by E. Crawford in Berlin wools. *Ulster Museum*

172 BERLIN WOOL WORK. The Finding of Moses in the Bulrushes worked in Berlin wools. Finished in 1875. *Ulster Museum*

be seen in London's Bethnal Green Museum. Signed and dated "Mrs J. Morris fecit 1851", it is one of six Last Suppers shown at the 1851 Exhibition.

Particularly realistic is "Joseph Presenting His Father to Pharaoh" at the Victoria and Albert. The fur on Pharaoh's robe is worked in cut-pile wool, and his "jewels" worked in seed pearls, sequins and beads.

In the Newark Museum, New Jersey, is a fine "Abraham Offering Isaac", signed and dated "Wrought by Dorcas Fiske Ashton aged 70 1843". The Bowes Museum has the "Anointing of David", the City Museum, Stoke-on-Trent, another Abraham and Isaac, while "Joseph Sold By His Brethren", "The Finding of Moses in the Bulrushes", and "The Pharisee and the Publican", are among Ulster Museum's collection.

Queen Victoria's pets and the Royal Family in general were favourite Berlin wool subjects, with the Prince of Wales in highland dress a particular one.

Floral subjects were used for upholstery and fire-screens, often over-size blooms depicted with great naturalism. The height of achievement was reached by means of elaborate shading, so that the flowers appeared to stand out from the ground in high relief, as the peonies and water lilies do in the chair-back in the collection of the Red House Museum and Art Gallery, Christchurch.

115

174 BERLIN WOOL WORK. Nineteenth century. The Prince of Wales in Highland dress, worked in Berlin wools. (The version in the Victoria and Albert Museum has him with his foot resting on a dog.) *Christopher Sykes Antiques*

173 BERLIN WOOL WORK. Nineteenth century. The Pharisee and the Publican worked in Berlin wools by C. O'Reilly. The colourings are raspberry red, moss green, brown and royal blue. *Ulster Museum*

175 BERLIN WOOL WORK. Roses worked in Berlin wools with a bead edging. *Christopher Sykes Antiques*

176 BERLIN WOOL WORK. *c.* 1830. Romantic Woodland Scene. *Ulster Museum*

116

177 BERLIN WOOL WORK. Parrot and blooms worked in Berlin wools. The bird is in plush stitch which gives it a three-d effect. *Embroiderers' Guild permanent collection*

117

178 BERLIN WOOL WORK. *c.* 1840. Parakeet and flowers in Berlin wools (unfinished). *Ulster Museum*

This realism was frowned upon by Lockwood and Glaister in their treatise on *Art Embroidery* 1878; this at a time when the work was still popular, but the art needlework movement was beginning to rear is head

> It is impossible to reproduce the odour of flowers [in needlework] as it is to imitate the bloom of their texture, the delicacy and evanescence of their more brilliant tints, or the minute details of their form. . . .
> The gaudy obtrusiveness of the Berlin-wool flower groups is owning to a mistaken apprehension of this very thing, and a desire to imitate natural appearances which are not capable of imitation. Such attempts are at best coarse and clumsy. . . .

Plush stitch was used to create the 3-D effect, which was a series of loops which were afterwards cut to give the effect of a thick velvet pile. The shearing was carefully graduated to emphasize the lines of a flower, the fur of a robe, or the plumage of a bird.

Gaudy parrots with their brilliantly exotic plumage looked marvellous worked in the brightly coloured Berlin wools using plush stitch.

An interesting method of working a star pattern in plush stitch is given in the 1885 guide to the worktable:

> Before beginning a pattern the worker must practise the stitch, which is suitable for footstools, cushions, etc.; it is worked with Berlin wool over strips of cardboard. The stars are worked with one colour only; the easiest plan is to mark them out on the canvas either with needle and wool or with pen and ink; commence in the narrowest part. Work three cross-stitches each over two ordinary stitches of canvas perpendicularly (see upper part of design), place a strip of card a quarter of an inch in width and an inch and a half in length over the

179 BERLIN WOOL WORK. Mid-nineteenth century. Panel for firescreen in Berlin wools with the cockatoo in plush work. *Victoria and Albert Museum*

180 BERLIN WOOL WORK. Early nineteenth century. English. A gamekeeper in a rural setting worked in natural colourings. He has a bright red waistcoat and a brown jacket. *Embroiderers' Guild collection*

stitches, fill into the shape of star, working over the card. The stars are separated by stripes of five shades of wool worked horizontally over eighteen stitches of canvas in the longest part and twelve in the shortest. Work the stripe from the point of one star to the point of the next after working the stars.

For the shaded stripe, begin with the darkest shade and work the row of cross-stitches and first row of plush-stitch with it. After working the cross-stitch, take a strip of card, place it over the row of cross-stitches, work over it for the plush-stitches as shown in the upper part of the design in exactly the same way as you would work herring-bone-stitch, working through two threads of canvas in a straight line each time. Work the second shade over the first, working into the next row of canvas threads (see design); continue working each shade over the last until the stripe is the width required.

Count the stitches for the next stripe, commence in the centre, and work the second stripe as described for the first. When all the rows are worked, take a pair of sharp scissors, insert them under the stitches just above the cardboard in the centre of the stripe, and cut through the wool. Great care must be taken in cutting the shape of the star, as the cutting may much improve it. When the cutting is finished (and there is great art in this to make the work look really well) hold over the steam of boiling water, and afterwards hold by the four corners and paint the back with strong gum to fix the stitches.

Artificial flowers were also made in Berlin wools – large overblown blossoms. The

119

181 BEADWORK. *c.* 1850. Cushion cover in multi-coloured beads on red velvet. *Bowes Museum, Barnard Castle*

182 BEADWORK. *c.* 1870. Tea cosy cover (unfinished). Grey and white beads on red silk. *Bowes Museum*

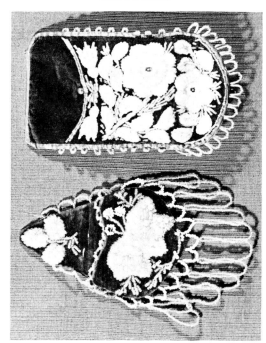

183 BEADWORK. *c.* 1875. Fan in highly coloured Berlin wool with white and grey beads with red fringing. *Bowes Museum*

184 BEADWORK. *c.* 1880. Watch pocket (one of a pair), and a "hussife" with white and glass beads (padded) on deep blue velvet. *Bowes Museum*

120

185 BEADWORK. *c.* 1890. Tray in grey and white beads on a blue ground of beads. *Bowes Museum*

186 BEADWORK. *c.* 1890. Both sides of a bead bag in bright naturalistic colours on blue and white grounds. *Bowes Museum*

187 BEADWORK. *c.* 1890–1910. Dress front of gun-metal glass beads highlighted with jet. *Bowes Museum*

188 BEADWORK. North American nineteenth century. Called an Ojibwa bandoleer bag with polychrome beads on black cloth in a design of flower and leaf shapes. The lower edge of the bag ends with four decorated strips each having two loops of blue and black glass beads at the base. *Embroiderers' Guild collection*

shapes of the petals and leaves were made of bent wire, or canvas mesh, and worked over in Berlin wools in their natural colours. The curved petals were "darned" backwards and forwards. Knotted wool threads were used to represent grass.

Sprays of flowers were put in large vases, or even under glass domes like wax fruit flowers, while some woven flowers were used as a border to decorate the edge of mats. (For an illustration of the wool flowers look back to a picture of wax fruit in chapter two, which features the flowers as well.)

Mediaeval romantic subjects can be found in Berlin wool work. Copies of Landseer's "Chevy Chase". "Bolton Abbey in the Olden Time", and various country scenes abound. A charming early nineteenth-century picture of a gamekeeper in a rural setting surrounded by his quarry and dogs, worked in natural colourings, with the gamekeeper in a brown jacket and red waistcoat, is in the Embroiderers' Guild collection.

Berlin patterns had a long life, which makes them a problem to date. Because the original pattern was so expensive to produce, it was either passed on to other needlewomen or sold back to the supplier, who then resold it probably at half-price or less. So there is usually no way of telling whether a particular picture was embroidered at the beginning or end of a pattern's life.

As a general guide, early floral designs tended to include small flowers like poppies and auriculas, whereas by 1850 the bigger exotic blooms and overblown rose were popular.

If Prussian blue is the predominant colour, it is safe to assume that the article was made after 1870.

As in needlework pictures, a clean finish, not too much fading of colours, good quality work, and an appealing design, are the best guide lines for the collector.

Another variety of Berlin work combined the use of coloured-glass **beads**; these were imported from Germany and Italy. They were sold by weight, so were known in England as *pound beads*. Small, tube-shaped beads of transparent glass were called *bugle beads*, and large cylindrical beads of opaque glass were called *O.P. beads*.

Banner fire-screens were embroidered with beads and Berlin wools, seat covers and backs for "prie-dieu" chairs (those chairs with a low seat and long straight back with a short horizontal top on which to rest the arms during prayer), and numerous small beaded items such as fans, bags, tea-cosy covers and bell ropes, photograph frames, slippers, pin-cushions and watch pockets and dress fronts. The choice for the collector is large.

A useful guide to dating Victorian beadwork is given in *Bead Embroidery* by Joan Edwards, who gives a detailed date chart.

The Embroiderers' Guild has an interesting collection of North American bead bags. A nineteenth-century bag is in red woollen cloth with polychrome bead work in the design of a tree with floral motifs. It is edged with black tape and white beads. Another one is known as an Ojibwa bandoleer bag with bead embroidery, and little clusters of beads decorating the end of the bag, which has four narrow strips at the base.

Reference to this North American beadwork gives me a chance to mention other

189 TABLE MAT. 1863. Probably Ojibwa Indian. In birch bark, cloth bound, strung-bead-edged mat decorated with porcupine quills and backed with brown velvet. Each quill is pushed once into the bark at each end. *Pitt Rivers Museum, Oxford*

190 DISH. Nineteenth century. Ojibwa Indian. Ornamental dish of birch bark with dyed moose hair embroidery in human and bird forms. *Pitt Rivers Museum, Oxford*

191 CASES. 1860–1870. Huron Indians of Lorette. Top, probably a sewing-case of green corded silk with base and top of birch bark. The top forms a lid of four overlapping pieces. The bark is edged with white moose hair oversewn with commercial cotton and decorated with "true" embroidery in dyed moose hair. Bottom row L to R semi-cylindrical birch bark case with "true" embroidery in dyed moose hair (before 1872); case for visiting cards etc., in birch bark covered with black cloth, the moose hair embroidery being stitched through the cloth into the bark, and the edges of the case piped with mohair couched in commercial cotton ; another case similar to the other, only in red cloth. *Pitt Rivers Museum, Oxford*

123

192 FISH SCALE EMBROIDERY. Believed to be English but made in the West Indies, 1891. Satin satchel embroidered in narrow silk braid, chenille thread, and in the centre, roses with fish scale petals and thread centres. *Bethnal Green Museum*

193 FISH SCALE EMBROIDERY. The other side of the satin satchel with more fish scale roses. *Bethnal Green Museum*

194 FISH SCALE JEWELRY. Brooch and ear-rings made from fish scales from Barbados, 1881. *Bethnal Green Museum*

124

Ojibwa Indian work in which strung-bead edging was used to decorate some souvenir items of the mid 1800s.

Honeymoon couples visiting Niagara Falls in 1863 could buy birch-bark table mats, cloth-bound with an edging of white strung-beads. The mats were decorated with porcupine quills – each quill is pushed once into the bark at each end. The mat was backed with brown velvet.

Another Victorian tourist souvenir is an ornamental birch-bark dish with dyed **moose hair** embroidery featuring bird and Indian figure motifs. These were said to be made by the Ojibwa Indians from Michigan.

The major decorative interest here is the moose hair embroidery, which is believed to have originated with three nuns of the Ursuline Order who landed in Quebec in 1639 to open a seminary for Indian girls; two more nuns joined the trio the following year. Three of the five were skilled embroiderers, and although at first the nuns used silk and thread sent over from home, this was obviously rather costly, so eventually local materials such as Indian moose hair was used.

Trinkets of birch bark decorated with moose hair, quills and beads became, from about 1714 onwards, a lucrative source of income for the convents. Not until the early nineteenth century did the Huron Indians of Lorette, Quebec, take over the lead in the market, with the Cayuga Indians (one of the Six Nations of the Iroquois) acting as "middlemen" at Niagara Falls and elsewhere.

Some of the small souvenirs made by the Huron Indians included such best-selling lines as small cases for visiting cards, and small cylindrical cases which were probably for cigars; all were in birch bark decorated with moose hair embroidery, the edges of the cases piped with moose or horse hair oversewn with commercial cotton.

All these items, as well as many others made by Indians for their own domestic use, are in the collection of the Pitt Rivers Museum in the University of Oxford. The expert there on both hair and quill work is Geoffrey Turner. His book *Hair Embroidery in Siberia and North America* is a fascinating detailed history.

In his book Geoffrey Turner says that to be suitable for use as an embroidery medium a hair must combine certain characteristics by no means common to those of all mammals:

It must be long enough for easy handling; thick enough to be readily visible; white, or only very lightly pigmented, so as to accept dyes; and capable of being folded, flattened or creased sufficiently to obscure the thread used for stitching. This near plastic quality is perhaps the most important of all, and certainly the least frequently encountered.

He sent me the photographs of the birch-bark items as representing the sort of hair-embroidered items that are most likely to be found in antique shops; they were also specially chosen to illustrate the visual difference between quill and hair, which are frequently confused.

"Compare the greater size and rigidity of the quills with the fineness and flexibility of the hairs)", he points out; and adds:

Quillwork trinkets were sold to tourists all along the St. Lawrence, and examples do turn up in antique markets, especially the cylindrical boxes (sometimes nested one inside another), which are generally ascribed to the Micmac Indians of New Brunswick, although other tribes also made them.

There are two birch-bark cigar cases to be seen at Blair Castle, seat of the Dukes of Atholl; these were brought back from Montreal as presents in 1863 by the Marquis of Tullibardine, son of Anne Hume Drummond and later 7th Duke of Atholl.

As this is rather a novelty chapter, it seems the best place to include embroidery which incorporated **fish scales**.

It was popular in the latter part of the nineteenth century, and the fish scales were used to imitate the petals, feathers and segments of a butterfly's wing.

Barbara Morris who is assistant Keeper of Circulation at Bethnal Green Museum, which has several examples, writes about it in the fancy-work chapter of her excellent *Victorian Embroidery*:

The fish scales had to be prepared before use and the iridescent scales of the carp, perch or goldfish were considered the most suitable. They were scraped from the fish with a knife, and steeped in cold water until soft and pliable, and two small holes were pierced with a needle near the base of each scale.

The scales were then coloured by a mixture of varnish and powdered colour after which they were ready to be sewn on to the ground (silk, satin or velvet), by silk thread, and were arranged in overlapping patterns to represent the petals of flowers such as roses, or the shapes of birds and butterflies.

Stems, veins, tendrils and other fine details were worked in fine chenille thread, gold thread or filoselle. The centres of flowers were filled in with French knots worked in silk or with pearls, glass beads or spangles.

The work in Bethnal Green which shows the use of fish scales is a satin satchel (1891), embroidered in narrow silk braid, chenille thread, and, of course, some fish-scale rose petals with thread centres. It is thought to be English, but made in the West Indies.

Rather unusual are a brooch and earrings made from fish scales from Barbados (1881) and an earlier brooch (1860) made of the scales of the Callipeva (Mugil Liza) from the West Indies.

10

Natural with the Needle

SAMPLERS
ART NEEDLEWORK
WILLIAM MORRIS AND LEWIS F. DAY
NEEDLEWORK SCHOOLS AND GUILDS

"Gardening with silk and thread"

Hints on Pattern Designing 1881
WILLIAM MORRIS

You need to be selective about samplers, those cloths on which a collection of miscellaneous stitches and patterns in embroidery were used as a reference in future work. The derivation of sampler is from the Latin *exemplum*, meaning anything selected as a model for imitation, a pattern, an example.

In the late fifteenth and early sixteenth century no printed patterns for needlework existed, so the expedient needlewoman embroidered a cloth as an *aide-mémoire* to record designs as an example to copy from.

Early samplers were real works of art, often over a yard long, less than a quarter of a yard wide, adorned with as many as thirty different patterns of lace and cut and drawn work. As they were narrow they could be rolled on a little ivory stick like the Japanese *kakemonos*.

Early samplers are rare, and if you want something different then you could concentrate on **map samplers**, which came into fashion in 1800. Patterns for maps were published during the 1790s which were obviously intended for adult work, and later they were sold printed on silk or linen grounds to be worked in delicate silk embroidery.

Many of the map samplers are enclosed by a floral border, often oval in shape, embroidered with a greater variety of stitches than could be used in tracing the map. The same flowers appear on the **darning sampler,** which also had its heyday around 1800. These samplers were decorated with petals of fine darning, worked with silk in two colours, on a very fine linen or woollen canvas.

The sampler is the first record of needlework in America, and the earliest samplers followed English patterns. As in England, they were made by both adults and children. The earliest and best known sampler is that made by Ann Gower, the wife of Governor Endicott. She made it in England in about 1610, and it is now in the USA – in the collection of the Essex Institute in Salem.

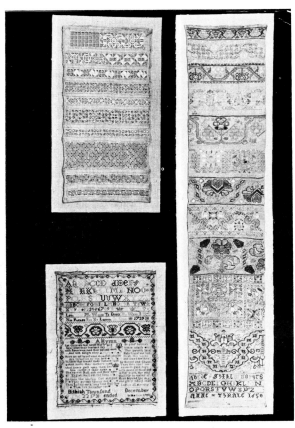

195 SAMPLERS. Group of fine samplers (top left). Early Stuart. Silk on coarse linen in drawn work, *c.* 1660. Signed "R" in top left hand corner. (Right) Irish. One of the earliest known dated samplers. Silk on brown linen. Signed and dated Anne Thrale 1650. (Bottom left) Silk on linen, signed and dated British Townsend 1740. *City Art Gallery Bristol*

196 SAMPLER. *c.* 1790. English. Oval map sampler, embroidered in coloured silk on linen with embroidered floral spray surround. *City Museums Stoke-on-Trent*

By the mid 1700s samplers included figures and houses, animals and plants, as well as an inscription of some sort and perhaps an alphabet or two. On a sampler dated 1776 in the Smithsonian Institute a Molley Russell worked her ABC, the refrain "When stern affliction waves her rod", as well as two figures and a border of flowers.

"Solomon's Temple" was a favourite subject in both Britain and America. As Averil Colby points out in *Samplers Yesterday and Today*:

> In many examples the building is accompanied with inscriptions giving the biblical proportions . . . all are large buildings, some surrounded by railings . . . handsome as they were, the designers' ideas on the architecture seems to have been somewhat shadowed by thoughts of the Brighton Pavilion or Victoria mainline railway station.

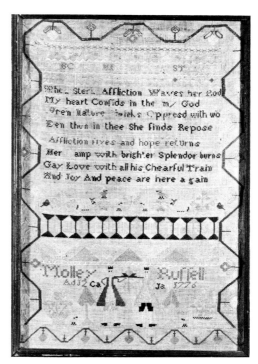

197 SAMPLER. *c.* 1850. English. Map sampler embroidered in soft-coloured silks on tammy cloth. *The Bowes
Museum*

198 SAMPLER. American. Worked by Molley
Russell, dated 1776. *Smithsonian Institution, Washington DC*

The inclusion of a coronet or crown motif into a pattern might have meant that it was worked in a noble household, or might have been put in just for decorative purposes.

An obviously popular motif in American samplers is the American eagle, and buildings of the period 1826; New York City Hall is featured on a sampler in the New York Historical Society collection, while the Crystal Palace was a favourite in England after 1851.

The inscriptions and verses, usually in sententious refrain – "Each fleeting moment of your time improve" . . . "Teach me to quit this transitory scene, with decent triumph and a look serene" and the like – were obviously on the lips of every child. An interesting collection of different rhymes could be built up by collectors.

Berlin wool work gave the sampler its final fling. Some were quite intricate, with the stitches varied and complex, and were not the work of children. Donald King in *Samplers* says of them: "Their purpose is not clear, but it seems possible that they were worked by skilled needlewomen to serve as models for amateurs, in the same way as coloured charts."

But as Mrs Head points out in her *Lace and Embroidery Collector*; "The introduction of Berlin printed patterns for cross-stitch, and Berlin wool with which to work them, dealt the sampler its death blow."

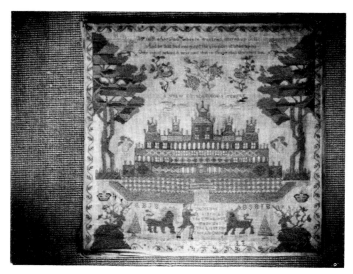

199 SAMPLER. *c.* 1800s. "A View of Solomon's Temple". Note the coronets on either side, and the lions at the base of the sampler. *Christopher Sykes Antiques, Woburn*

200 SAMPLER. Worked 1841. English. Unusual design with a central motif of a large bouquet of flowers, surrounded by butterflies, birds and flowers. Note the coronet worked over the owner's name Susannah Tillier. *E. Tudor-Hart, Brighton*

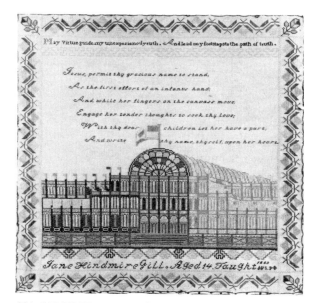

201 SAMPLER. 1853. Showing Crystal Palace. *Bowes Museum*

202 SAMPLER. 1832. English. Framed work "Wrought by Frances Smart". *Ingram Warwick Antique Lovers' Coterie*

203 SAMPLER. 1828. English. *Bowes Museum*

204 SAMPLER; 1800. English. *Bowes Museum*

205 SAMPLER. 1800–1850. English. *Bowes Museum*

206 SAMPLER. 1822. English. *Bowes Museum*

207 SAMPLER. 1880. English. Worked in Berlin wools by Sarah Elliott. *Bowes Museum*

209 EMBROIDERY PANEL. 1897. English. "The Flowerpot" panel designed by William Morris and worked by his daughter May Morris. Coloured silks and gold threads on linen and lined with cambric. *William Morris Gallery*

208 EMBROIDERED WALLHANGING OR PORTIERE. 1887. English. Silk embroidery designed by Henry Holiday and worked by his wife Catherine. They were friends of William Morris who commissioned Mrs Holiday to work for him. The central motif is a palm tree in a green vase, against a background of flowers—chrysanthemum, tulips and lily. Mrs Holiday died in 1924 and this piece was kept in the family until 1971, when it was sold at auction through *Sotheby's, Belgravia*

210 SCREEN PANEL. 1890. English. Designed by May Morris daughter of William Morris. Large shaggy tulips in shades of cream and pink with deep green leaves with a coral background worked in heavy floss silk on a loosely woven linen. Surface darning throughout except for stem stitch outlines. *Embroiderers' Guild collection*

211 VICTORIAN WOMEN AT LEISURE. Working with wool.—'Total collapse of our decorative needlework?' asked Lady Marion Alford in 1886. *Radio Times Hulton Picture Library*

As Berlin work superseded the sampler, so it in turn received its death knell from **art needlework**. Caulfield and Saward's *Dictionary of Needlework* (1882) described this phenomenon as

> a name recently introduced as a general term for all descriptions of needlework that spring from the application of a knowledge of design and colouring, with skill in fitting and executing. It is either executed by the worker from his or her designs or the patterns are drawn by a skilled artist.

The surge of interest in needlework is credited to William Morris (1834–96), the designer and craftsman whose work is considered the most important single influence on the development of late nineteenth-century decorative art.

In 1861 his firm, Morris, Marshall, Faulkner and Company opened in Red Lion Square as "Fine Art Workmen in Painting, Carving, Furniture and the Metals". He also designed (among many other things) wallpaper, fabrics and embroideries; one of his early commissions was for a frieze for the dining-room of Rounton Grange, North Allerton, the house built by architect Philip Webb for Sir Lowthian Bell. It

212 VICTORIAN WOMEN AT WORK. "Needlework as an art is as dead as the proverbial door nail. The death-knell rang for all time when the sewing-machine was invented . . ." Mrs Emily Leigh Lowes 1908. *Radio Times Hulton Picture Library*

213 Books on Art Needlework. *Author's collection*

was designed by Morris's great friend Edward Burne-Jones in 1874 and featured scenes from Chaucer's *Romaunt of the Rose*. Although Burne-Jones designed the figures, Morris obviously had a hand in the background, for it was a combination they continually used when working together. The frieze is now at the William Morris Gallery, Walthamstow, a place for the Morris *aficionado* to visit.

There is more, much more, one could write about Morris, but there are whole books devoted to this brilliant man among whose friends were Ruskin and the big names of the Pre-Raphaelite brotherhood, Rossetti and Holman Hunt.

Morris's pioneering work, together with that of the Church embroidery societies, led to the formation of a number of societies specifically devoted to the promotion of needlework. The most famous is the Royal School of Art Needlework founded in 1872 by two talented embroideresses, Miss Helen Welby and Lady Marion Alford, with Princess Christian (Queen Victoria's third daughter) as royal patron.

In her book *Needlework as Art* (1886) Lady Marion also had a dig at the decline of needlework during the middle of the eighteenth century. Praising the work of a Mrs Pawsey, who ran a school of needlework at Aylesbury patronized by Queen Charlotte, she insisted; 'This was out last attempt at excellence, immediately followed by

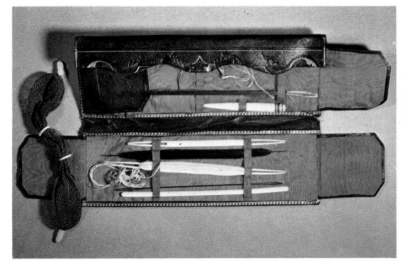

214 NETTING TOOLS. Early nineteenth century. Tooled leather case containing netting needles etc. in bone and metal. At the side is a netted "miser's purse" which has a central slit opening and "toe" ends to hang down from a belt. The metal rings were for securing the coins in the "toes". *Red House Museum and Art Gallery, Christchurch*

215 NETTED PURSES. Nineteenth century. Three netted and bead purses with a miser's purse on the right. The steel-beaded long purse is *c.* 1850–1860. *Red House Museum and Art Gallery, Christchurch*

216 BOX OF COLOURED BEADS. Early nineteenth century. A selection of beads used for making net purses and bags. *Red House Museum and Art Gallery, Christchurch*

217 EMBROIDERY FOR CARD TRAY. The tray was fitted into a light frame of gilt reeds by means of blue silk cord and tassels. Three triangles were cut out of cardboard, covered with white cloth and lined with taffeta. *Art Needlework, 1883*

are embroidered with crewels or split filoselle in four shades of pink, and the blossoms with

47.—WRITING-CASE.

48.—GARDEN BASKET.

49.—EMBROIDERED TABLE. FOR DETAIL SEE NO. 43.

50.—DUSTER BASKET.

51.—DETAIL OF NO. 50.

white.   The wheatears are worked in chain stitch with maize-coloured filoselle or crewel wool

218 PAGE FROM ART NEEDLEWORK. 1883. English. What to make. The writing case was covered with bronze plush on the outside, with the same coloured satin inside. The top was embroidered with a monogram, and the lining for the lid had a satin ribbon sewn in loops for the writing utensils to go in. The garden basket was of Roman straw, fitted with a bag netted with écru-coloured thread and drawn up with cord and tassels. A bouquet of flowers was embroidered on the basket. The duster basket was of willow and black polished cane, ornamented with three plush vandykes, joined together and finished with woollen bulb, tufts and tassels. The plush was embroidered all over, and the design outlined with gold cord. The low trefoil-shaped table was covered with crimson satin, edged with heavy cord and fringe, and embroidered all over.

the last total collapse of our decorative needlework, and the advent of the Berlin wool patterns.''

In its turn art needlework also got out of hand. Mrs B. Townend in *Talks on Art Needlework* calls it ''a womanly occupation, and it is wonderful how many pretty, and really beautiful and artistic things can be made for the adornment of our homes, and our persons, out of very little. . . .''

Therein lay the trouble. Everything, but everything, from baskets (work, duster, waste-paper) to furniture (garden, footstool, whatnot), was *smothered* in embroidery.

136

219 ADVERTISEMENT FROM ART NEEDLEWORK.
1883 : *Liberty Art Fabrics*

How could you embroider a whatnot? No problem – the details were given in *Art Needlework* (1883), "a complete manual of embroidery in silks and crewels". After you finished the embroidery, a scalloped band which presumably hung round the shelves, you finished off the job "with cords, tassels, and bows in passementerie".

The book is rather a chamber of horrors – writing cases, tables, mats, fans – all encrusted with the delights of the needle – collectors' pieces if only as a reminder of the industry of our Victorian ancestors.

Yet the book also decries "the era of Berlin wool work which has happily passed away . . . worthily consigned to oblivion" and pours scorn on the "terrible things entitled 'fancy work'. . . Alum baskets, cardboard constructions, wax flowers – would any of these serve to delight future generations?" asked the anonymous author.

"Art Needlework?" queried Lewis F. Day (1845–1910) in his *Art in Needlework* (1900), summing up the whole thing; "It has helped to put an end to the patience of the modern worker, and to inspire her too often with ambitions far beyond her powers of fulfilment. . . . We plume ourselves too much upon our art. . . ."

In 1906 the Embroiderers' Guild was formed to promote a high standard of work and design; it still flourishes, and a recent magnificent display was called "One Thousand Years of Embroidery" which was most informatively catalogued by Lynette de Denne. The guild has branches all over Britain and associated societies in the USA.

As this is not a book on the history of international embroidery I will only refer in passing to a couple of the big names of the needlework world in America, Mrs Candace Thurber Wheeler (1828–1923), and the more recent Georgiana B. Harbeson.

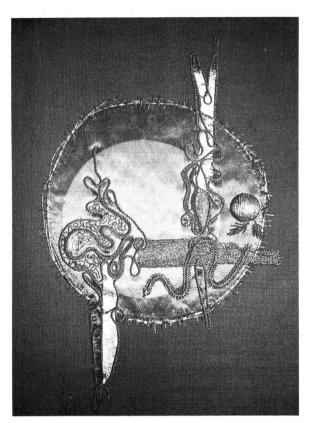

221 THE BARONNE DE VEAUCE. Formerly Miss
Burton of Upton Court, Slough. Needlework revived.
"While her husband, who is a great musician, plays to
her she occupies her evenings in this remote place (Cha-
teau de Veauce, near Vichy, France), by embroidery."
Notable Needleworkers' feature in *Needlecraft Monthly
Magazine,* 1908

222 SAMPLER. Contemporary. American. Drawn and
pulled thread work on white linen with fringed end.
Bucky King Embroideries Unlimited, Pittsburgh, Pennsylvania

Sufficient to say that from their efforts must have grown what Bucky King of Embroideries Unlimited Pittsburgh calls "the hard, steady backbone of our stitchery movement".

In an article in a recent issue of *Embroidery,* the excellent magazine of the Embroid-
ers' Guild, she tells of a group of American artists and designer craftsmen in stitchery,
who have chosen needlework as their medium of expression: 'They are constantly
designing and creating to produce new combinations . . . deeply committed to stitchery
as an art form."

The work of members of this group which includes Anna Ballarian, David Van
Dommelen, Nik Krevitsky, Jean Ray Laury and others, will become collectors' pieces
too, as exciting experiments in textile decoration.

Bucky King herself designs and executes interesting pieces using metal thread and
appliqué, plus the more traditional drawn and pulled thread work.

Back in Britain there are also numerous embroiderers breaking away from

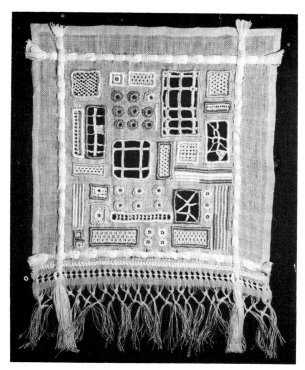

224 FABRIC PICTURE. Contemporary work by Ellen Cunningham "Maelstrom". The "waves" are polythene, the maelstrom itself gold kid, the background black rayon crepe mounted on winceyette. *Modern Embroidery Group Glasgow School of Art. Exhibition Foyles Art Gallery*

223 METAL THREAD WORK. Adam and Eve in metal thread a technique used by Bucky King. *Embroideries Unlimited, Pittsburgh, Pennsylvania*

picturesque florals and landscapes. Their work is a vital, creative means of expression, something intensely personal, giving needlework a sculptural, three-dimensional feeling. There is a touch of collage too, about the materials they use – net, string and Lurex, raffia, straw, seed pods, hessians and the like.

Ellen Cunningham, who trained at the Glasgow School of Art (which gave a new direction to teaching embroidery way back at the turn of the century), creates pictures that are a combination of embroidery and collage. "Maelstrom" has glassy "waves" of polythene, carefully cut to overlap in definite forms, and outlined in gilt or silver thread. The actual turmoil is mainly composed of imitation kid, interspersed with pieces of real gold kids in varying shades. There is very little glueing in the panel, and the threads used for sewing are silver, gold and Lurex. The black background is of dressmaking rayon crêpe mounted on winceyette to prevent "slip".

When I bought "Maelstrom" at an exhibition by the Modern Embroidery Group of the Glasgow School at Foyles Art Gallery, the artist said that she hoped that I could live happily with it. I have to admit it is not easy – there is something faintly disturbing about it, as there is obviously meant to be. It is a restless piece, somewhat overwhelming, yet typical of our age, exciting and vital; not a dead creation, but something alive.

11

Tools of the Trade

DRIZZLING FOR SILVER AND GOLD
NETTING, KNOTTING AND TATTING
WORKBOXES, THIMBLES, NEEDLES AND THE LIKE

*"Technical excellence in needlework, as in all other artistic crafts, is a question
of the worker's perseverance and her ability in the use of tools."*

Embroidery and Tapestry Weaving
MRS ARCHIBALD H. CHRISTIE 1906

Imagine being at a party attired in your best gold and silver braid, complete with
fringes and tassels, and suddenly finding that the other guests were snipping bits off
to sell to the highest bidder!

This actually happened to the Duc de Chartreu sometime in the 1780s! It was
described in some detail in Madame de Genlis's novel *Adèle et Théodore*, published
in France in 1782, and drew attention to the peculiar hobby of **parfilage**, known later on
in England, when it was brought there by the refugees of the Revolution, as "drizzling",
a name no doubt inspired by the incessant "tsrr, tsrr, tsrr", that accompanied the job
of ripping and unravelling threads being torn apart.

The *parfileuses* were not only carrying out their occupation as a social pastime. They
were able to sell off their bounty! Trimmings of gold and silver were extremely valuable, since they consisted of real gold and silver wrapped round an inner cope of
silk. Once unpicked, the threads were returned to the lacemen, usually the tradesmen
who had supplied the original items, who paid handsomely for them, as they in turn
sold them back to the goldsmiths and silversmiths who melted them down for the
valuable metal of which they were made.

Naturally not all the unravelling was carried out when the unfortunate person was
actually wearing his glory. Discarded military uniforms, lavishly trimmed and embroidered women's dresses of an earlier decade, servants' old liveries – all were seized upon
for the treasure they afforded.

The *parfileuse* would carry a pouch containing the necessary tools. In the City of
Sheffield Museum you can see a set of French eighteenth-century drizzling implements, in a case of silver and blue enamel, with holes through which cord would
go to hang it from the waistband; in it are a drizzle pin and thread knife, both
for unpicking, with steel blades and engraved silver handles, plus a pair of scissors.

140

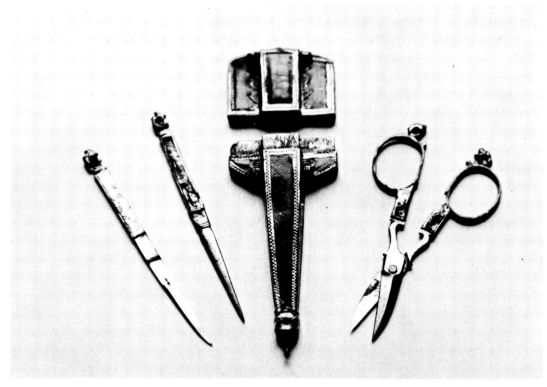

225 DRIZZLING SET. Eighteenth century. French. Case of silver and blue enamel containing drizzle pin, thread knife and scissors. *City of Sheffield Museum*

Men indulged in the hobby too. Prince Leopold, widower of Princess Charlotte who died in childbirth, used his wife's tortoiseshell drizzling box. He made enough money from it to buy a silver soup-tureen for his niece Princess (later Queen) Victoria.

Leopold used to drizzle away when he visited his lady-love, well-born German actress Caroline Bauer, who quite rightly complained that at the sound of this detestable drizzling she wanted to scream – he had the temerity to sit there drizzling when he came to call on her, when he could have been making love!

Drizzling sets are rare, but there must be some of the implements around, only waiting to be recognized.

Also in sets come **netting** tools, complete with needles and gauges. Netting, which ranged from fishermen's nets, women's handkerchiefs and mob caps to curtains, was described in the late 1800s as "this beautiful work which has long been fashionable because of its strength and durability".

Mrs Delany remarks that she "found the Duchess of Portland busy making a cherry net of 100 meshes per row".

I rather like the idea of a netted night set for which instructions were given in

141

226 NETTED BEAD BAGS AND PURSES. Nineteenth century. Miscellaneous bags and purses. *Harris Museum and Art Gallery, Preston*

a Victorian women's magazine. It was "particularly recommended to persons who suffer from headaches as it [presumably the night cap] keeps the hair closely together without any pressure on the head".

Netted and **bead bags** were popular towards the end of the nineteenth century, and are attractive to collect; particularly "miser" purses, which were tiny narrow netted containers with a central slit opening and "toe" ends, to be carried or worn on a belt. Two metal rings could be slid from the centre over the slit to secure the coins in the toe.

The practice of **knotting** thread or cord for use in embroidery was known in Britain in medieval times, but really got under way at the end of the seventeenth century. The thread needed was first wound on a shuttle and by means of this a series of picots or knots was made in it at close intervals, so that it formed a narrow trimming

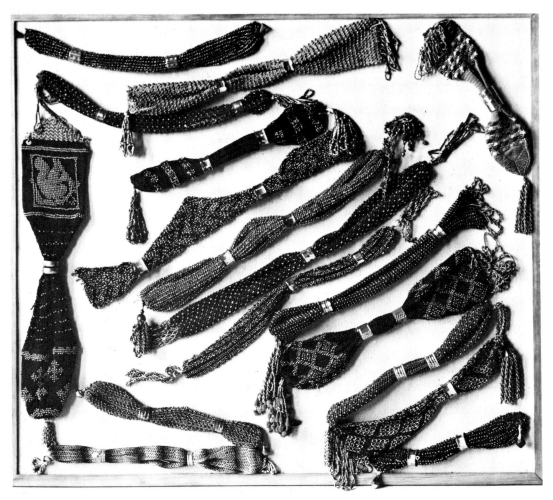

227 NETTED AND BEADED PURSES. Nineteenth century. Various shapes and sizes of miser purses. *Harris Museum and Art Gallery, Preston*

looking a bit like a string of beads. Afterwards it was couched down in patterns on to linen or other fabrics.

A knotting shuttle is formed of two oval blades pointed at both ends and joined in the middle. With her usual one-upmanship, Mrs Delany naturally indulged in knotting, and had a knotting shuttle in gold, a present from George III in 1783, "of most exquisite workmanship and taste".

Princess Amelia, daughter of George II, was also reputed to be fond of knotted work, and a panel of knotting which she may have worked with the Duchess of New-asch is in the Embroiderers' Guild permanent collection. It was found in small pieces by Ruth, Countess of Chichester, and restored and repaired by her between 1955 and 1959.

Likely to be available to the collector are shuttles made of ivory, bone and horn

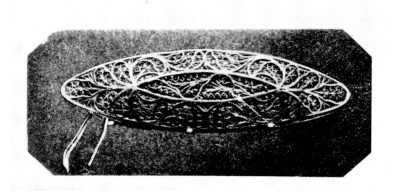

228 KNOTTING SHUTTLE.
Eighteenth century. Believed to be
Mrs Delany's; she had a large
collection including one that was
a present from George III.

229 KNOTTING. A bag covered
wih knotting work done by Mrs
Delany.

(some inlaid with shell), while others are in wood, painted and veneered, porcelain, mother-o'-pearl and tortoiseshell.

The transition from knotting to **tatting** was a gradual one. The object of knotting was, basically, to provide a decorative line or cord for appliqué in surface embroidery. Tatting, although using a similar technique, created patterns and trimmings complete in themselves. The shuttles were small and pointed, and were in ivory, pearl, bone, vulcanite and tortoiseshell.

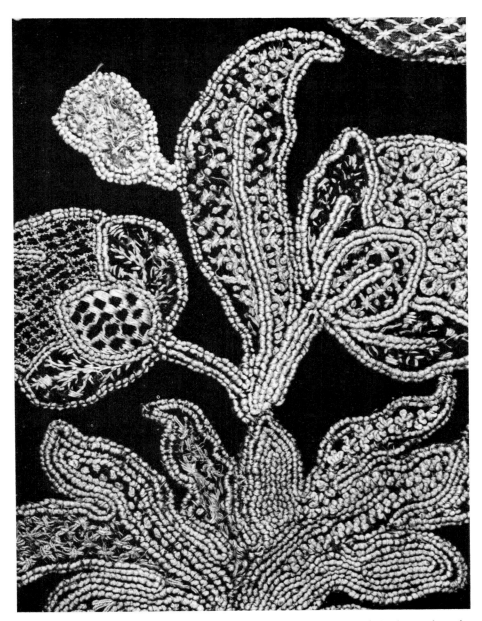

230 KNOTTING PANEL. English mid-eighteenth century. Part of the knotted work reputed to have been worked by the Duchess of Newasch and Princess Amelia daughter of George II, also Lady Chichester, later first Countess of Chichester. It was found in small pieces by Ruth, Countess of Chichester. Mended, repaired and reassembled on to dark brown linen by her during 1955–1959. The work comes from Halland the Sussex home of the Duke of Newcastle. Écru coloured linen threads are knotted and couched down with some surface stitches originally worked on to mid-brown linen.
Embroiderers' Guild collection

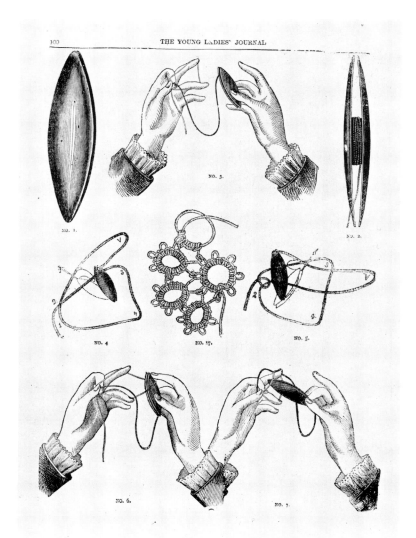

231 TATTING. A step-by-step guide on how to thread a tatting shuttle.
The Complete Guide to the Work-Table,
1885

The English word "tatting", incidentally, could come from the French *tâter* to touch. The feel or touch of the stitches (single, double and picot), passing through the fingers was sufficient to tell you, after a little practice, if it was being done correctly. In Italy, where tatting was said to have originated in the sixteenth century, the work was known as *occhi* from the eyes or rings of which it is made up.

The Complete Guide to the Work-Table (1885), referring to tatting as "not mysterious in progress like knitting", advised that

attention should be paid to the shuttle being well made, so that the brass pins which fasten one part to the other should not protrude and render the shuttle difficult to draw through.

To thread the shuttle, you will find there is a hole, pierced through the centre piece; pass the cotton through this hole, and tie a knot only just sufficiently large to prevent the thread from slipping, then wind your shuttle full.

146

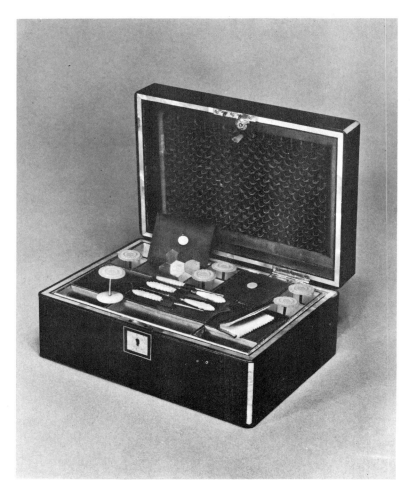

232 WORK BOX. Nineteenth century. Wood with mother-of-pearl trim containing reel holders, needle case and a piece of patchwork. *Ingram Warwick Antique Lovers' Coterie*

233 SEWING ACCESSORIES. (left to right) nineteenth-century finger shield; seventeenth-century Dutch thimble; seventeenth-century German thimble and needle case; English silver thimble and vinaigrette 1790; Chinese finger guard (*London Museum*). *Embroiderers' Guild History of Sewing Tools reprinted from Embroidery Magazine*

234 LA MÈRE LABORIEUSE. "The Industrious Mother" print after a painting by Chardin (1699–1779) in the Louvre. Note the pincushion box in the corner by the dog. *Radio Times Hulton Picture Library*

148

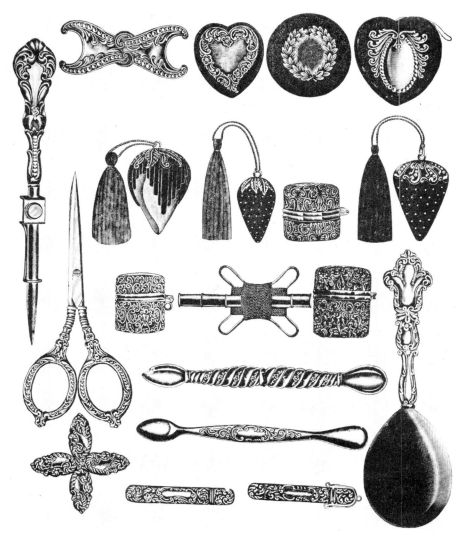

Then came a step-by-step guide on how to make a work-basket ornamented with tatting. The basket was of gilded wicker, lined with peacock blue satin, and each side was ornamented with a deep-pointed drapery composed of tatted rosettes. The tufts in the centre of the rosettes were made with Berlin wool and gold thread over wire, and the handles of the basket ornamented with clusters of woollen balls. Need I say more?

Mid-eighteenth-century **workboxes** would contain writing implements as well as needlework tools. They were not always actual boxes either, but pouches and the like. Mrs Delany in 1779 was given by Queen Charlotte a "most beautiful pocket case, the outside white sattin work'd with gold and ornamented with gold spangles . . . lined with pink satin, and contains a knife, sizsars, pencle, rule, compas and bodkin", and so on.

236 SEWING ACCESSORIES. (top) Miniature chest of drawers for holding cottons, with a pincushion top; (right) cotton reel stand on a small box with a drawer below; (left) needle-woman's clamp which was fixed to a table to hold a piece of material firmly for working on; the top is a pincushion and there is a drawer for needles and thread. *R. B. Dickson*

Larger in size and more ornate are the workboxes in the shape of a spinet, still to be found, but costly. Most of these spinet-boxes, popular in the early 1800s, have a music box incorporated in the "keyboard" end; the fittings are usually of silver, elaborately chased and ornamented.

A sewing box in bird's-eye maple in the American Museum at Bath was made for Mrs Benedict Arnold, wife of the notorious General. It was made by Elsabar, a Mic-mac Indian; the accessories include a birch-bark needle case, on the flyleaf of which, in faded ink, is a message the simple Indian woman wrote to Mrs Arnold, dated October 7, 1791.

237 INSTRUMENT FOR MAKING TWISTED CORD. This appliance enabled the worker to make any kind of twisted cord. It was a small metal instrument and the three small discs are wheels, supported on the arms of an upright cross which has a heavy circular base. These three wheels were connected by a cord with a layer wheel below that has a handle attached to it. The cord runs in a groove round the circumference of each wheel, and had to be held taut in position. By turning the handle of the large wheel the three small ones were set in motion. Three hooks, attached to the axles of the small wheels, were therefore rotated with them. One end of each ply of the cord being made, was looped on to one of these hooks; the other ends were attached to three similar hooks fixed into a block of wood which, when in use, was firmly clamped to the table. *Embroidery and Tapestry Weaving, Mrs Archibald H. Christie 1906*

Such conclusive dating evidence is, of course, rare. Locks sometimes give a clue in dating a box. Box locks with link plates (i.e. the closed type of catch as against the hook type) and inlaid key escutcheons usually mean late eighteenth-century origin. Handles can be helpful as they often follow the furniture styles of the period.

Needle-pushers, **finger shields** and **guards**, and **thimbles** all did much the same sort of job. The German for a thimble is *fingerhut* which translated means finger hat; in French it is *dé* and Spanish *dedal*, both derived from the Latin word meaning finger. The English thimble comes from the Anglo-Saxon *thymel* (in turn related to the German *daumen*, meaning thumb), and it was originally a small bell-shaped cap of leather, made to be worn on the thumb when sewing.

Throughout the years thimbles have been made from an enormous variety of materials, including gold, silver, glass, porcelain, bone, rubber and wood. The field is wide for the collector.

In the 1700s thimbles often served a dual purpose. They were combined with scent flacons; engraved with a monogram and used as a seal; screwed on to a pair of scissors, or formed the base of stiletto.

China thimbles were made in the mid nineteenth century; and the few that bear the maker's mark are those from the Royal Worcester factory.

think my readers will be interested if I give them some information as to the tools used, how, and what, to buy in order to set about the work.

I have had to use the French words for the tools, as I do not think they are made in England—though the ones used for leather work are very much the same, and could also be used for lead.

The work ought to be a favourite with ladies for several reasons, amongst which are that it neither hurts the hands nor makes a noise (except one uses nails, when, of course, there is the little tapping sound, but this is not a necessary part of the work). It is also very inexpensive. An artistic effect can easily be produced without difficulty, and before much skill is acquired, though in the higher branches of the work much artistic taste is needed.

To enumerate the things for which it can be used would take all my space, but the following are a few : Boxes of all kinds, from large chests such as were used for armour in olden times, to pin or match boxes ; overmantels, frames, covers for books, blotters, hat pins, buttons ; and a little while ago I saw a most wonderful bedstead, which had its two ends ornamented with étain and brass work. Indeed, every day one discovers new things which can be made with it.

The material is bought in sheets at about 6s. a yard. It must be absolutely pure lead (without alloy), or it will not yield to the working, and will probably cut. This latter catastrophe is what is most to be dreaded, and often occurs to the beginner.

The tools are few and inex-

Hammer.   Spadule.   Pied de Biche.   Modeleur.
Tools for Étain Work.

I should advise a beginner to furnish herself with four—the "Spadule," the "Modeleur," the "Pied de Biche," and the little hammer.

Now comes the choice of what is to be made. A match or a pin box is perhaps the easiest to begin with. They can be bought in white wood, but a cardboard box such as a chemist uses in which to send out his powders, does very well when no brass or copper is inserted, nor nails used, all which pertain to a higher branch of the work, of which I hope to speak later.

Next comes the choice of pattern. A simple little flower with one or two leaves will be quite sufficient to show what may be done.

Stones can be inserted in the middle of the flower, and to form berries.

The sheet of lead will be seen to have a bright and a dull side. The worker can choose either on which to model the design. The bright side can be burnished to look like silver, but I must confess to a leaning to the dull face, as when finished the work looks more like old pewter.

The pattern for the covering of the box must now be cut out exactly in paper. This is then laid on the sheet of lead, and with an ordinary pair of scissors the étain is cut out, leaving a very tiny margin for overlapping. The lead ought to cut quite easily, and this is one of the tests of its being pure.

The design is then drawn on the paper, and when laid exactly on your already cut out piece of lead, the design is traced with the "pied de biche," or a blunt pencil, so that the pattern is quite distinct, making an indented line on the lead. This tracing must be firmly done, but little pressure used.

When the paper is removed the design must be gone over again with the "pied de biche," so that a good line is shown, but great care must be taken not to make a hole.

Now turn the étain over, and with the flat end of the spadule press out the parts which ought to stand out in relief. This will require going over several times, as it must be done with a gentle touch, and the higher parts *gradually* modelled. The "Modeleur" can be used for stalks and veining of leaves. Turn the work again

A Casket and Photograph Frame decorated with Étain. Nails and Jewels are also used.

238 ÉTAIN WORK. Tools for étain work, a process of decorating sheets of lead which was used to form boxes, photograph frames and so on. The finished effect looked a little like pewter.
Needlecraft Monthly 1906

Thimbles often had their own little cases lined with velvet, and many Victorian thimbles were made for children and can be found in sets, that is, several thimbles of varying sizes fitted inside each other.

If you wanted a **needle** of a particular size in Victorian days, you used a dial-a-needle box. Such a one was a Paris knick-knack written about in *The Queen* magazine of March 1888 :

The top of the box is ornamented with embroidery on plush. It is movable, turning as it does on a pivot. The numbers (1, 5, 10, 15, 25 and 50 on a centre panel) serve to indicate the size of the needles contained in each compartment.

Another novelty, a do-it-yourself one this time, a fan needle-case and pincushion, was in *The Queen* of 1887.

Any palm or Japanese fan may be utilised for this purpose, or any handscreen, cut out from a piece of stiff cardboard and covered with some fancy material, with the addition of a gilt or enamel painted stick.

An old battledore or tennis racket may be turned to account, and prettily adorned with loops and ends of pompadour ribbon.

The book of flannel leaflets, in which the needles were stuck, had pinked-out edges and was attached to the centre either with sewing or a long fancy pin.

A **pincushion**? There is a wide range in both dates and styles for the collector. In 1729 Mrs Delany (then Mrs Pendarves) wrote "Mrs. Dashwood junior is as well as can be expected considering her condition; I have got her pincushion to stick for her." For the fashion was to decorate large heart-shaped or rectangular pincushions with pins inserted in such a way that they spelt out a greeting such as "God Bless the King and Queen" or "Welcome to the Royal Babe". The industrious mother, *La Mère Laborieuse*, as painted by Chardin, was never still.

Other novel sewing accessories to search out are **emery cushions** filled with emery powder for polishing rusty needles (a silk "strawberry", for instance, the outside of which would be used as a pincushion, would be filled with emery); **silk winders** (small, flat and pointed for winding off lengths of thread); **clamps** (which could be fixed to a table to hold a piece of material firmly to work on); and revolving **cotton-reel stands**, which you can still use today to store your cottons on.

An unusual item, illustrated in Mrs Archibald Christie's *Embroidery and Tapestry Weaving*, was an instrument for making twisted cord, an ingenious appliance composed of three small wheels, with hooks attached to their axles, rotated by turning the handle on a large wheel. "Simple as a toy to handle, giving excellent results", said Mrs Christie, in her 1906 practical textbook of design and workmanship. Also in this useful little book are drawings of a cutting knife, to be used in an upright position, with the point outwards; a spindle for winding gold thread upon while working; and a piercer, also for use in gold work.

Although we are now well into the twentieth century with our collecting, and the reign of Edward VII and Alexandra in full swing, the inventiveness and industry of Victorian times is still in evidence. Although women's magazines were decrying what they called "Victorian monstrosities". the home craft workers were still as busy as ever.

"The traditions of craft and design are not dead, and the revival has come in time, one would think, to fan into flame, what has only been slumbering", pointed out the *Needlecraft* magazine of 1908 giving instructions for embossed leather work, silvered and lacquered; thonged leather work, punched and fringed; *étain* or lead *repoussé* work – you could cover everything from a book to a bedstead with it – all was grist to the mill of the eager handicraft worker.

Of *étain* work the description went:

The work ought to be a favourite with ladies for several reasons, amongst which are that it neither hurts the hands nor makes a noise (except one uses nails, when, of course, there is the little tapping sound, but this is not a necessary part of the work). It is also very inexpensive. An artistic effect can easily be produced without difficulty, and before much skill is acquired, though in the higher branches of the work much artistic taste is needed.

What more suitable final words for a craft book? Happy collecting to you. . . .

What to Read

Collage and Fabric Pictures

Fabric Pictures by Eugenie Alexander. Mills and Boon 1963
Embroidery and Fabric Collage by Eirian Short. Pitman Publishing 1967 and Metuchen
   N.J., Textile Book Service.
Starting Fabric Collage by Frances Kay. Studio Vista 1969

Flowers and Leaves

Bottle Gardens and Fern Cases by Anne Ashberry. Compton Printing 1965
Pressed Flower Pictures by Pamela McDowall. Lutterworth 1970
Pressed Flower Collages by Pamela McDowall. Lutterworth 1971

Hairwork

Hair Embroidery in Siberia and North America by Geoffrey Turner. Oxford University
   Press 1953

Macramé and Knotting

Varied Occupations in String Work by Louisa Walker. Macmillan 1896
Square Knot Handicraft Guide by Raoul Graumont & Elmer Wentstrom. Cornell Maritime
   Press USA 1949
Introducing Macramé by Eirian Short. Batsford 1970
Macramé, Creative Knotting by Imelda Manalo Pesch. Sterling Publishing Co. 1970
Macramé Made Easy by Eunice Close. John Bartholomew 1973

Needlework

American Needlework by Candace Wheeler. New York 1921
Early American Textiles by Frances Little. New York 1931
American Needlework by Georgiana Brown Harbeson. Coward McCann, New York,
   1938
English Historical Embroidery by Barbara Snook. Batsford 1960
Victorian Embroidery by Barbara Morris. Barrie & Jenkins 1965
Historical Needlework by Margaret H. Swain. Barrie & Jenkins 1970
Guide to English Embroidery by Patricia Wardle. H.M.S.O. 1970
American Crewel Work by Mary Taylor Landon and Susan Burrows Swan. Collier-Mac-
   millan 1971
Discovering Embroidery of the Nineteenth Century by Santina Levy. Shire Publications 1971

Needlework Boxes and Tools

History of Sewing Tools. Embroiderers' Guild 1967
The History of Needlework Tools by Sylvia Groves. Country Life 1968
Old Needlework Boxes and Tools by Mary Andere. David & Charles 1971

Paper Work and Silhouettes

Small Antique Furniture by Bernard and Therle Hughes. Lutterworth Press 1971 (Chapter on paper filigree work)
British Silhouettes by John Woodiwiss. Country Life 1965
Silhouettes by Peggy Hickman. Cassell 1968
Women in Profile by F. Gorden Roe. John Baker 1970
British Profile Miniaturists by Arthur Mayne. Faber 1970
Papercutting by Brigitte Stoddard. Batsford 1972

Patchwork, Quilting and Appliqué

Quilts and Counterpanes in the Newark Museum, Newark, New Jersey 1948
Quilts, Their Story And How To Make Them by Marie D. Webster. Tudor Publishing Company, New York, 1948
American Quilts And Coverlets by Florence Peto. Max Parrish 1949 & Chanticleer Press, New York
The Standard Book of Quilt Making and Collecting by Margaret Ickis. Constable 1959 & Dover Publications, New York
One Hundred and One Patchwork Patterns by Ruby Short McKim. Constable 1962 & Dover Publications, New York
Patchwork Quilts by Averil Colby. Batsford 1965
Patchwork Today by Doris E. Marston. G. Bell 1969
Patchwork for Beginners by Anne Dyer. Booklet National Federation of Women's Institutes 1969
Old Patchwork Quilts and the Women Who Made Them by Ruth E. Finley. G. Bell 1970 & Charles T. Bransford Company, Newton Centre, Massachusetts
Patchwork by Averil Colby, Batsford 1970 and Newton Centre, Mass. Branford
Notes on Applied Work and Patchwork. Victoria & Albert Museum
Exploring Patchwork by Doris E. Marston. G. Bell 1972
Appliqué by Evangeline Shears and Diantha Fielding. Pitman Publishing 1972 and Watson-Guptill Publications, New York

Samplers

American Samplers by Ethel Standword Bolton and Eva Jonston Coe. Massachusetts Society of the Colonial Dames of America, Boston 1921
Guide to the Collection of Samplers and Embroideries by F. G. Payne. 1939

British Samplers by Mary Eirwen Jones. Oxford 1948
Samplers by Donald King. H.M.S.O. 1960
Samplers Yesterday and Today by Averil Colby. Batsford 1964

Shells and Sand

The Shell Book by Julia Rogers. Charles T. Branford, Boston 1951
American Seashells by R. Tucker Abbott. D. Van Nostrand, New York 1954
Shells of the New York City Area by M. K. Jacobson and W. K. Emerson. Argonaut Press, Larchmont N.Y. 1961
The Romance of Shells in Nature and Art by Louise Allardice Travers. M. Barrows & Co. New York 1962
Shellcraft by Anthony Parker. Stanley Paul 1963
Collecting Shells by S. M. Turk. Foyles 1966
Shell Collecting by S. Peter Dance. Faber & Faber 1966 & University of California Press, Los Angeles 1966
Sea Shells of the World with Values by A. Gordon Melville. Charles Tuttle Co. 1967
Van Nostrand's Standard Catalog of Shells. Princeton 1967
Collecting Sea Shells by F. D. Ommanney. Arco Publications 1968
British Shells by N. F. McMillan. Frederick Warne 1968
Coloured Sands of Alum Bay. Official Guide. P. Cray 1969. Borough Press
Discovering Sea Shells by Barry Charles. Shire Publications 1971
Shells by Roderick Cameron. Octopus Books 1972

Straw Work

Decorative Straw Work by Lettice Sandford & Philla Davis. Batsford 1964
Prisoners-of-War Work 1756–1815 by Jane Toller. The Golden Head Press 1965

Tatting

The Craft of Tatting by Bessie M. Attenborough. G. Bell 1972

Tinsel Pictures

Penny Plain Two Pence Coloured by A. E. Wilson. G. Harrap 1932

Waxwork

Modelling Wax Flowers by John & Horatio Mintorn. 1844
Art of Modelling Waxen Flowers Fruit etc. C. G. W. J. Francis 1851

156

Miscellaneous

Mrs. Delany at Court and among the Wits by R. Brimley Johnson. Stanley Paul 1925

Antique Collecting For Everyone by Katherine Morrison Mclinton. Bonanza Books, New York 1951

Decorative Arts of Victoria's Era by Frances Lichten. Bonanza Books, New York 1950

Regency and Victorian Crafts by Jane Toller. Ward Lock 1969

Useful Addresses

The Embroiderers' Guild 93 Wimpole Street, London W.1

J.E.M. Patchwork Templates Forge House, 18 St Helens Street, Cockermouth, Cumberland. Tel. Cockermouth 2224

United States of America Embroiderers' Guilds:

Cleveland Branch Mrs Crandall Stark, 11005 Fidelity Avenue, Cleveland Heights 44111

Colorado Embroiderers' Guild Mrs George W. Wilson, 7564 Moore Court, Arvada, Colorado 8002

Hinsdale Embroiderers' Guild Mrs Paul Carson, 114 East Walnut Street, Illinois 60521

Pittsburgh Craftsman Branch Mrs Earl F. McClune, 400 Mohawk Drive, Mount Vernon, McKeesport, Pa 15135

Oklahoma Mrs Charles D. Iddings, 4221 E. 41st Street, Tulsa, Oklahoma 74135

Tallahassee Handweavers and Embroiderers' Guild Mrs J. C. Moore, 2109 Evergreen Drive, Tallahassee, Fla 32303.

Virginia Mrs L. I. Thomas, 2016 Hanover Avenue, Richmond Avenue, Va. 23220

Royal School of Needlework 25 Princes Gate, London S.W.7

Bucky King Embroideries Unlimited, 121 South Drive, Pittsburgh, Pa, USA

Needlework Textile Guild Chicago, Illinois, USA

Needle and Bobbin Club New York, USA

New York Shell Club meets Sunday afternoon at the American Museum of Natural History

Eaton's Shell Shop 16 Manette Street London W.1

Index of Names and Subjects

Index of Museums, Art Galleries and Organizations

161

162